Exploring the Joy of Christmas

DUCK COMMANDER®
FAITH & FAMILY FIELD GUIDE

Exploring the Joy of
CHRISTMAS

STORIES, RECIPES, CAROLS & MORE
from the Stars of A&E's *Duck Dynasty*

PHIL & KAY ROBERTSON

with Bob DeMoss

REGNERY
FAITH

Regnery Faith™ is a trademark of Salem Communications Holding Corporation; Regnery® is a registered trademark of Salem Communications Holding Corporation

Duck Commander® and its logo are registered trademarks of Duck Commander Inc.

Scripture taken from the Holy Bible, NEW INTERNATIONAL VERSION®, NIV® Copyright © 1973, 1978, 1984, 2011 by Biblica, Inc.® Used by permission. All rights reserved worldwide.

Cataloging-in-Publication data on file with the Library of Congress

ISBN 978-1-62157-481-1

Published in the United States by
Regnery Faith
An imprint of Regnery Publishing
A Division of Salem Media Group
300 New Jersey Ave NW
Washington, DC 20001
www.Regnery.com

Manufactured in the United States of America

10 9 8 7 6 5 4 3 2 1

Books are available in quantity for promotional or premium use. For information on discounts and terms, please visit our website: www. Regnery.com.

Distributed to the trade by
Perseus Distribution
250 West 57th Street
New York, NY 10107

To our sons, daughters-in-law, grandchildren, and great-grandchildren, all of whom bring Christmas joy to us 365 days a year.

Contents

Acknowledgments

Hat tip goes to our good friend Bob DeMoss for helping us tell the story, to our new friends at Regnery Faith—Marji Ross, Mark Bloomfield, Katharine Spence, Maria Ruhl, John Caruso, Emily Bruce, and Patricia Jackson—as well as our old friends Mel Berger and Margaret Riley King at William Morris Entertainment. We're eternally grateful to the Father, Son, and Holy Spirit for making Christmas something to celebrate.

1

Memories and Mistletoe

I know what it is to be in need, and I know what it is to have plenty. I have learned the secret of being content in any and every situation, whether well fed or hungry, whether living in plenty or in want.

PHILIPPIANS 4:12

Our exploration of finding the true joy of Christmas starts with a heart of contentment regardless of our circumstances. You might want to read that again. Miss Kay and I have discovered what it means to be content no matter what. We have been so poor there were many Christmases when we didn't have enough to eat—unless we went out and plucked food up from the ground, picked it off of a tree, or shot it from the sky. On the other hand, we've benefited from a thriving duck call business and television show. Through all of that we've learned a thing or two about joy.

At the top of the list is this undeniable fact: true joy is a gift that Jesus gives when He changes our hearts. Once that happens, regardless of our lot in life, we'll be good to go. All we have to do is keep our eyes on Him—not on the stuff this old world peddles. Hey, there isn't a kitchen appliance, flat screen TV, cellphone gadget, or piece of clothing that can bring you lasting joy. I see them yuppies whipping out their platinum credit cards buying everything in sight thinking their purchases will make them happy, happy, happy. When the bill comes due, get back to me on how that joy is working out, see what I'm saying?

Personally, I avoid the mall at Christmas at all costs. But then again, I avoid the mall during the rest of the year, as well. Masses of shoppers clogging the aisles on the hunt for a good deal make me *nervous*. I'd much rather do my hunting down by the river where it's peaceful and quiet. That said, Miss Kay and I thought it'd be a slick idea to invite you into our home to see what we did do over the years to maintain a spirit of contentment. Hey, you'll see a little redneck engineering can go a long way when times are lean.

Hunting for the Perfect Christmas Tree

Americans spend more than $1 billion on Christmas trees, fake or real, each year. I get mine for free. I just go and chop one down. They don't get any fresher than that. You say, "Where do you find one to cut?" That's simple. I have probably traversed every creek there is in northern Louisiana. I've covered just about all of them either on foot or I've paddled 'em in a pirogue—that's a long, narrow canoe for you citified folk. I always keep a sharp eye out for the makings of a great Christmas tree and then make a mental note of the location.

I know all of the good spots. I've been doing that since my childhood. Admittedly, I've learned there's a right and a wrong way to go about that. Not long after I had become a Christian, Miss Kay, Alan, and I went out to fetch us a tree—not at a lumberyard or department store like they do in Yuppieville. Since times were hard and we didn't have any money, we walked through a thick patch of trees where I had spied one earlier. Miss Kay didn't recognize the area so she said, "Now, Phil, we're not cutting down a tree where we shouldn't be cutting, are we?"

"No, no. We can't be doing that," I said. Several moments later I heard the engine of an approaching pickup truck. I was like, "Everybody get down!" We all hit the dirt. I've never seen Miss Kay move that fast. While she was on the ground, she said, "Okay, why are we hiding if it's okay for us to get the Christmas tree here?"

"Well, I thought it was okay. Maybe we shouldn't be here," I said, clearly busted.

"Hey, if you're having to hide out when you get your Christmas tree," Miss Kay said, standing up and dusting the dirt off of her jeans, "you're probably taking it from someplace you shouldn't be." I'll admit as a new Christian I was still a little bit shaky on some things. Now that we own a few hundred acres, I no longer have that temptation, see what I'm saying? And, now that we have a little extra money, we're able to just buy one if I don't want to fool with that whole lumberjack scenario.

Either way, we usually get our tree during the first week of December. Miss Kay keeps it up in the house into January. You say, "Why not just buy a fake one and use it year after year?" Nope. There's nothing like the smell of a fresh tree. And Miss Kay has a field day decorating it. Always has. When we had no money, she'd find a way to beautify the tree with Spanish moss or garlands handmade out of popcorn and cranberries. The last twenty years we've gone for more of a hunting theme where she'll string together shotgun shells—not live ammo, mind you, spent hulls—duck decoys, and such. I hear tell you can buy them that way these days.

We just made them ourselves.

I mean to tell you, nobody beats Miss Kay in the Christmas decorating department—even back when we had no money. We'd go into the woods to gather magnolia leaves and all kinds of outside plants and pinecones. She'd spray-paint them with two dollars' worth of silver or gold paint and then mix them up with some fresh-picked red holly. You might say the woods was our Walmart. That's a fact. Hey, we'd even forage for things in the dump. It wasn't always trash. We found all kinds of Christmas decorations, like a set of little reindeer someone had thrown away.

The dump was our flea market back then.

GAG GIFTS, CALCULATORS, AND PEANUT BUTTER SANDWICHES

Phil is the hardest person on the planet to buy a present for because he's so particular. Besides, he has no interests outside of hunting. None. He usually asks for something that's hunting related, like a knife. Nobody ever bought him clothes in fifty years unless it was socks—which he rarely wears anyway. About ten or fifteen years ago, I decided that if I can't buy Phil something he wants, I'll get him a gag gift. That tradition has turned into buying gag gifts for everyone.

Courtesy Phil and Miss Kay Robertson

Come August, I'll spend hours in the bookstore buying the gag gifts. Take Vinny Mancuso who married Alan and Lisa's daughter Alex. Since he's in the family and he's Italian, I'll buy something Mafia related. I'll put on his card, "Vinny, I got some stuff from your family history and thought you might enjoy it." I bought Jase a book something like *101 Positive Sayings for the Negative Person.* Jase was like, "Why would you give me this? I'm not negative."

I got Missy *101 Ways to Cook Bacon.* The fact of the matter is that Missy despises bacon. She thinks the fat is no good for you. That year I gave Willie a Richard Simmons *Sweatin' to the Oldies* video workout on DVD. He about died. I laughed so hard when I gave Phil a book on the Russian opera. He was like, "Miss Kay, why in the world would you get me that?" Or the time I bought him the memoirs of Bill Clinton. Any time there's a liberal politician like Harry Reid or Nancy Pelosi, I'll get Phil something from them. Or I'll buy something from a sports team they hate, like the banner I bought Alan from Notre Dame—a team that he can't stand.

One year I bought Alan fake dog poop because he always gags when he smells dog poop. We used to have so many dogs around the house, we went through a period of time where every Christmas somebody would track dog poop inside. We'd have a massive shoe search to figure out who was the culprit. Sometimes I made them all leave their shoes outside—and then the big dogs would take 'em and chew them to pieces.

More than anything, the key to the gag gifts for me is watching the reaction. I get so thrilled about it. Sometimes I'm so tickled I start laughing and I can't get out the story why I bought them that gag gift. They get so tickled over me trying to stop laughing that we all end up laughing until we cry. Even Alan has gotten into the gag gift–giving action. He recently bought Phil a decorative plate with Barack Obama on it.

I wouldn't be surprised if Phil "accidently" drops and breaks it one day.

I'm sometimes asked what's the most memorable gift Phil has bought me. People are surprised when I tell them that Phil, for the most part, is not a gift giver. That might upset a lot of women, especially at Christmas. It never upsets me. I couldn't care less, and that's the truth. Sometimes Phil will think of something to get me and deputize one of the boys to pick it up. It ain't him traveling out to the mall—malls make him *nervous*. There was one exception to that.

Something like forty years ago, Phil actually went to JCPenney and bought me a new set of cookware...and a calculator. Hey, there's nothing like a good calculator to say "I love you," right? He got the calculator because it was my job to keep track of the money we didn't have. He even had the store gift wrap my gifts. You see, that was the Christmas Phil came to Jesus, and I think he wanted to make up for the fact that we had been separated for three months. He even stayed home Christmas morning instead of hunting that year like he usually did. He just wanted us to be together as a family.

More important than any gift Phil could get me is his Christian walk. He's the provider and the leader of the family. He has so many more good qualities that offset the fact that he doesn't go Christmas shopping. He trusts me to do that for him. Don't get me wrong. He does bring me wildflowers when he returns from a hunt from time to time.

I know he loves me!

Speaking of gift giving, when Willie was a youngster he gave me a half-eaten peanut butter and jelly sandwich—in a baggie—for Christmas. To him, that was a big deal. Food was tight, and we all know Willie likes to eat! Of course, I tried not to laugh. I don't think I succeeded. When the boys were older and had a little spending money of their own, the four of them chipped in and bought me a new KitchenAid mixer—the big one that sits on a stand all on its own, complete with all of the whisks and attachments.

I don't know whose idea it was to do this, but the boys put together an elaborate scavenger hunt that started with a big, heavy box. I couldn't believe my eyes when they lugged it out. I couldn't imagine what it was. When I opened it up, it was filled with rocks to make it heavy. On top there was a note with a clue for the next location—a jewelry box. I thought for sure they bought me some jewelry, only to find out there were more clues ahead—ten in all. They had me running all over the house hunting for my present...which ended up being hidden in the dryer. I had always wanted one of those mixers. I still have it today.

BLACK FRIDAY AND BLACK EYES

As Christmas approaches, there are two words that strike terror in my heart: Black Friday. You say, "Why, Phil?" Most people can't wait to hunt for the best deals. Good for them. I'm just afraid someone will try to drag me along with them. For the record, I don't like to shop... and I *despise* shopping on Black Friday. So does Miss Kay. She did it one time and then vowed never to do that again. She described how a couple of "ladies" came to fists in a literal fight in the store. Why? They were arguing over who got to be first in line. Good grief! For the life of me I can't figure that one out. I mean, we're supposed to be celebrating the birth of the Prince of Peace, right?

It's been my observation that in spite of my efforts to avoid a knock-down, drag-out fight by staying away from the stores, sometimes arguments end up on my doorstep over the holidays anyway. There have been more than a few throw-downs between several of our extended family members when they come to visit at Christmas. Hey, the Robertson side of the clan just loves to debate politics, philosophy, the Bible, or the best way to do this or that. Maybe that dynamic happens in other people's homes, too.

The way I see it, we should do everything in our power to maintain grace and self-control in every situation. After all, Jesus says, "Blessed are the peacemakers, for they will be called children of God" (Matthew 5:9). Did you catch it? Peacemakers are children of God— which makes sense. Since Jesus is the Prince of Peace, His children should seek the peace. That can be difficult when friends and family, whom you haven't seen in a while, gather together. It's almost inevitable for the bickering to start up, for someone to feel slighted, for feelings to be hurt—maybe even over a gift that was meant to be a gag, or over something you didn't get that you were hoping for.

As Miss Kay and I explore the joy of Christmas in this little field guide, the secret to a lasting joy isn't in the abundance of things that we have, that we get, or that we give. Here's a news flash: You cannot buy joy. Not today, not tomorrow—not at any price. That's what the Apostle Paul and Timothy were driving at when they wrote that verse in Philippians. Joy comes from a heart of contentment, and that comes from the Person whose birth changes everything. Hey, as you'll see in the next chapter, that's especially good news considering how many ways our plans for a special Christmas have misfired.

For to us a child is born, to us a son is given, and the government will be on his shoulders. And he will be called Wonderful Counselor, Mighty God, Everlasting Father, Prince of Peace.

ISAIAH 9:6

_____

Making the Most of Christmas Misfires

We Robertsons have had our share of what you might call "Christmas misfires." I'm talking about those minor disasters—like burning a pie or overcooking the turkey—and those little emergencies—like running out of a key ingredient—that spring up in spite of your best-laid plans. If you let 'em, those misfires can put a serious damper on your celebration. Over the years Phil and I have had to learn to roll with it when they happen so that our celebration isn't ruined.

For example, back when Granny and Pa were living next door to us on our property, we shared the Christmas cooking—this would have been between 1976 and 1990. We had both houses cooking up a storm because we'd have such a big crew, you know, with the extended family coming to join us. I'd be cooking up here in our house, and Granny would cook down the hill at her place while the family wandered between our homes sort of grazing, talking, and playing games.

Granny would make her sweet potato pies, her pecan pies, her fruit cake, and a big ham, much like you'd find at a traditional Christmas meal. I'd make a few appetizers, like my Festive Holiday Cheese Ball (see page 122), biscuits, cornbread stuffing, Broccoli and Rice Casserole (see page 130), and maybe a turkey and such. Keep in mind this was before we started our Cajun Christmas Extravaganza tradition. One year Granny announced she was going to roast this big boar. I'd cooked those before and thought it'd be a great idea. She put that thing in the oven and then started working on her other preparations.

As the boar was roasting away, maybe ninety minutes later, everyone who walked into her house noticed a horrible smell. I mean, it stunk *bad*—like something incredibly sour. That wretched thing smelled worse than a skunk trapped in a gym bag of dirty socks. The whole house stunk. That's when she realized she must of gotten an old, super stinky boar hog. We literally had to throw it out to the dogs. Guess what? Even they wouldn't eat it. That's how bad it smelled.

At that point we had to scramble to make something else for our hungry family and the relatives. These days you could buy a Heavenly Ham. But this was back in the days before you could run to the store and buy something preprepared. If anything we cooked went foul, or if we ever ran short on anything, we knew we could always eat fish. Phil would say, "Don't worry, Miss Kay. I'll go pick up a couple nets." He would clean the fish, we'd fry them up, and we'd be good to go.

The problem would come when Phil got a little heavy-handed on the spices.

I remember the year we ran a bit short on the main course. Phil pulled up some fish out of the river and cooked them for us. One problem: he got carried away and put *way* too much black pepper on the white perch. Everybody who was trying to work in the kitchen started sneezing, coughing, and wheezing. That's the truth. When the fish were cooked, I couldn't eat them. Phil tried to act like I was exaggerating about the spice. He told me that he ate seven pieces. But I noticed he left most of them uneaten on his plate. That's never happened in the history of him being here. Never.

If they were too spicy for Phil, they had to be *lethal*.

Here's another one.

About twenty years ago, in addition to the usual gifts we'd opened, I thought it'd be a sweet idea to give each of the boys and their wives fifty dollars cash in an envelope. That way they could spend it on whatever they'd like. Fifty dollars was a lot of money back then. Still is. Leave it to Alan to misplace his envelope somewhere in the mountain of gift wrap piled up in the living room after we opened the presents. To make matters worse, we used to carry the wrapping paper outside to burn it. We don't

Courtesy Russell Graves

burn it anymore, but in the old days that's just what you did. The best we can figure is that Alan's envelope got burned up along with the discarded paper. I was sick about it. I never gave them cash after that Christmas. Now I'll write them a check if I decide to go that route.

While smelly boars, blazing hot fish too spicy to eat, and a misplaced fifty-dollar bill are a couple of our Christmas misfires, they don't compare to a *literal* misfire... I'll let Phil tell that one.

BURNING DOWN THE HOUSE

About fifteen years ago, Miss Kay and I had an eight-hundred-square-foot addition put onto our home—which is the house you see if you watch *Duck Dynasty*. Up until we added the extra space, we raised our four boys in a space no bigger than 1,400 square feet—with one bathroom. Once Alan, Willie, Jase, and Jep got married and started bringing the grandkids over for holidays, we had a bit of a dilemma. Since we were tighter than a can of sardines, we scraped together the money for the addition. Problem solved.

With Christmas rapidly approaching, the builders did their best to get things wrapped up in time. In fact, the fireplace was finished maybe less than a week before Christmas. Since our tradition has been—and continues to be—to go duck hunting on Christmas morning for our main course, I invited Alan to hunt with me. He and Lisa and their two girls, Anna and Alex, came over Christmas Eve to spend the night. I want to say the girls were something like thirteen and eleven at the time. Jep was here, too.

I recall that Christmas we were hit with a massive ice storm, the likes of which we'd never seen in all of our years. The temperatures were so cold, everything froze. The way I figure it, somewhere along the line a tree must have fallen under the weight of the ice, knocking down the power lines. Bam! We had no electricity. None. These days if our electricity goes down, a big generator outside automatically comes on and our power continues—which is a pretty slick move, by the way.

But in those days we didn't have the money to buy a generator. With the electricity off, once it got dark we had to walk around with flashlights. There was not one ray of light—not even from the moon hidden behind the clouds. See what I'm saying? And, due to the freezing temperatures, we had no water. Making matters worse, since there was no power, we had no heat.

That's when I built a fire in our new fireplace for the first time.

Jep, the grandkids, and Miss Kay went to sleep on the couches near the fire. Alan and Lisa slept in the back bedroom since he was gonna get up early with me to go hunting. And, after stoking the fire and adding an extra log or two, I went and laid down in our bed. At three o'clock in the morning I raised my head off of my pillow because I thought I was smelling smoke. That's when I remembered I had the fireplace going in the main room since that was the only heat we had. I put my head back on the pillow and tried to fall back asleep. About five minutes later I got to wondering why I was smelling that much smoke. Grabbing my flashlight, I walked over to the family room.

Of course, Jep, the grandkids, and Miss Kay were sound asleep even though it was pretty smoky. I aimed my flashlight at the fireplace. The wood was just sitting in there smoldering. Not seeing anything unusual, I headed back to bed. I laid there for another five minutes and then thought, "Something's not right—something doesn't *smell* right." I got up, walked back in there armed with my flashlight, and bent down to study the hearth. You see, when that old redneck built the fireplace, he placed one layer of bricks right on top of a wood floor.

Now, I've never built a fireplace and have no plans to do so. But something didn't seem right where the bricks met the wood. Looking closer, I saw a little wisp of smoke. That got me to thinking: "Why would smoke be coming from underneath that brick instead of going up to the chimney? Why would smoke be coming out there in that crack?" Upon further investigation, I decided to fetch the water from one of our five-gallon water jugs we had stored in the kitchen. We had several of those in case our electricity went out and we didn't have water to cook with. I took a five-gallon jug of water and poured it right into the crack where I saw the smoke escaping.

The minute I did, the bricks and wood hissed.

And, the water started to boil.

Now, back in those days the closest fire station was all the way in West Monroe. It'd take them thirty or forty minutes to get out to our place—maybe longer due to the ice storm. Before I called them, I wanted to make sure this wasn't something minor. With the family still oblivious to the potential danger, I walked outside with my flashlight to look inside the crawlspace under our house. It's a tight space with three feet or so between the ground and the joists.

Mind you, with the exception of my flashlight it was pitch black as I crawled up in there. Looking in the distance where the fireplace was attached to the house, the first sign that we had a serious situation was the smoke hanging underneath my house. When I turned off my light, I saw a red glow coming from under the fireplace. I said aloud, "That sucker's on fire where the brick meets the wood."

That's when I hightailed it outta there. I got on the telephone and called my neighbor. I said, "Get over here. I think the house is on fire." He asked me to repeat what I said—after all, this was about 3:15 a.m. I said, "I'm not sure, but I think our house is on fire. Bring a chainsaw and a sledgehammer with you!"

He came tearing up the road and arrived within a minute. I grabbed that sledgehammer out of his hands and got to pounding on the bricks. I told him to grab more of the water jugs from our front porch, where we had a bunch of them stored. Of course, with all of that commotion going on, Miss Kay and the kids got up. With a yawn, she said, "What are you doing, Phil?"

I said, "I think this house is on fire."

Half-awake, she said, "What are you talking about?"

"I don't know. But I'm fixing to find out."

Meanwhile the kids started screaming and running around like their pants were on fire—which they weren't. But between me pounding on the bricks and smoke filling the air, they were scared. Hey, who wouldn't be, right? The fact that it was dark made things ten times worse. By this point Miss Kay, now fully awake, couldn't believe I was busting all of the bricks. She said, "What are you fixing to do?"

"I'm fixing to tear all of this out of here."

"Are you crazy? We just built that fireplace!"

"Trust me, honey," I said. "I know what I'm doing. We can always rebuild it."

I proceeded to knock those bricks on the hearth out of the way. Once I did, we could see that the whole floor underneath was just glowing red. I told everyone to start pouring water on it. Everyone started going crazy. Jep was running back and forth with those five-gallon jugs—even Miss Kay was lugging them as if her life depended on it. One of the women called the fire department. The whole scene was insane. I'm pounding away with the sledgehammer while they're scurrying around in the dark trying to bring the water fast enough to douse the flames.

JINGLE ALL THE WAY

Here's the funny part. While we were trying to save the house from burning down, Alan's oldest daughter, Anna, went under the Christmas tree and plucked out all of her gifts—nobody else's gifts, mind you. She went to rescue just her presents. She put them in a bag and took them outside to safety, which turned out to be the funniest part of the story. Nobody else thought about getting the Christmas gifts outta there because we were thinking the house was going to go up in flames.

Just after four o'clock, the fire department rolled in and quickly surveyed our fire situation, which, by that time, had been basically put out. The lead fireman walked over and said, "Mr. Robertson, most of the time when we respond to the report of a house fire it's completely out of control by the time we get there." He looked at Miss Kay and then back at me, adding, "What you just did with that sledgehammer and those five gallons of water saved your whole house—and probably your family, too."

I glanced at Miss Kay—who was still fuming that I had smashed her fireplace to smithereens—and had the good sense to hold my tongue. He said, "That was the move to make. Bust it and pour water on it."

Miss Kay was like, "Good grief. Don't encourage him." Hey, I don't blame her. We're talking about destroying the brand-new fireplace we had just added, something she'd never had in all of our days. There's one other part of the story worth mentioning. After the firemen departed the premises, Miss Kay asked me a pointed question: "Phil, what are you going to do now?"

Keep in mind it was just after four o'clock in the morning. Alan and I were planning on getting up at five a.m. to go duck hunting. I said, "Well, ain't no use going to sleep. I'll tell you what we're gonna do. We're going to go and kill us some ducks for Christmas dinner."

"Right now? Your house almost burned down!"

"Yup. And I put it out, didn't I?"

Pointing her flashlight around the room, Miss Kay said, "In case you didn't notice, there's all of this busted-out brick and wood, and there's mud everywhere from everyone traipsing in and out with those water jugs. And you're gonna leave?"

"Hey," I said with a shrug. "We'll get everything cleaned up when I get back. That mess ain't going nowhere." I'm pretty sure I saw a wisp of smoke form around the edges of her eyes as she gave me a look hotter than that old fire. Nevertheless, Alan and I put on our hunting clothes, grabbed our guns, and just tore out of there.

You say, "Phil, did Miss Kay ever forgive you for pulling a stunt like that on Christmas morning?" Yup. She admitted she was glad she had married a pioneer man—the kind of dude who wakes up in the middle of the night smelling smoke and who says, "Whew, that don't smell right."

Come to think of it, that was the only year we didn't have Christmas in our own home. We had to take all of the food, the shrimp and stuff that we were going to fry, over to Jase and Missy's house. But we found a way to get through even a misfire like that. Personally, I was happy, happy, happy that I didn't sleep through the early warning signs that could have caused the house—and all of us—to go up in smoke. Most people just sleep through it, see what I'm saying?

To this day I'm grateful that the Almighty spared us.

Today in the town of David a Savior has been born to you; he is the Messiah, the Lord.

LUKE 2:11

_____

3

The First Sunday of Advent

WHAT IF JESUS HADN'T BEEN BORN?

"Repent and be baptized, every one of you, in the name of Jesus Christ for the forgiveness of your sins, and you will receive the gift of the Holy Spirit. The promise is for you and your children and for all who are far off, for all whom the Lord our God will call."

Christmas is my favorite season—even ahead of duck-hunting season. You say, "Why, Phil?" At Christmas we celebrate the Almighty's decision to send a Savior, the One who brings hope and purpose to us little lumps of clay scurrying around planet earth. Think about it. Without the Christ Child, none of us have a prayer of making it to heaven. You might want to read that again.

Miss Kay can confirm that during the first couple of decades of our life together I was preoccupied with my selfish whims. Man, I was a first-class mess. I'm surprised she didn't give up on me back in my rompin' and stompin' days. Thankfully, the birth of Jesus changed all of that for me. If He can change my heart, He can change the heart of anyone who is willing to let go of their evil ways, too.

That's the power of the Christmas story.

I'd say that's worthy of celebrating, wouldn't you?

Have you ever wondered, "What if Jesus hadn't come to earth and we didn't celebrate Christmas?" "What if the angels never lit up the evening sky?" "What if they never announced to the shepherds the incredible news that the promised Messiah had finally come?" "Instead of Mary and Joseph welcoming their newborn baby, what if the manger was filled with nothing more than a few tired, raggedy old farm animals?"

I'm intrigued by the historical implications that go along with that line of questioning because I'm a "What if _____?" person. I've often considered how the course of history would have changed if just one person had acted differently. Put it this way: if one piece of information had been known, one decision had been made, or one action had been taken sooner rather than later, the outcome of any given event would have been very different.

With that in mind, let me direct your attention to Matthew 13. Here we'll explore several parables of Jesus's that lead us ultimately to the joy found in the greatest story ever told. Afterward, I'm gonna play the "What if _____?" game with those stories. Jesus begins with "The Parable of the Sower" (Matthew 13:3–23), which is about the obstacles in life preventing the "seeds of faith" from taking root in our hearts. He follows that one with "The Parable of the Weeds" (Matthew 13:24–30) in which an enemy intentionally sows weeds in order to ruin the harvest—and the fact that the good and bad plants will grow side-by-side until the day when they'll be sorted out, with the weeds being tossed into a "blazing furnace" (Matthew 13:50).

There's another parable, called "The Parables of the Mustard Seed and the Yeast" (Matthew 13:31–33). The idea there is that something very small, when blessed by God, can grow into something very great. That's what faith does in the hearts of people. Then we come to two little bitty short parables. In Matthew 13:44, Jesus says, "The kingdom of heaven is like treasure hidden in a field. When a man found it, he hid it again, and then in his joy went and sold all he had and bought that field."

You say, "Phil, why would anyone in their right mind hide the treasure again? If he found it, why doesn't he just go and celebrate? Finders keepers and all that, right?" I'll admit that's a little bit quirky for us with our twenty-first-century mindset to understand, especially if you're living in Yuppieville. You've got to remember when Jesus told the parable, He was talking to a crowd who lived in an agrarian society that had its own set of rules. If you're out working in a field, you're working for someone else—and whatever's in that field rightfully belongs to the owner.

What was His point? The only way the man could keep the treasure was to make the sacrifice of selling everything in order to buy the field and become the owner of that great treasure. Then, to drive home the message, Jesus added a second parable, saying, "Again, the kingdom of heaven is like a merchant looking for fine pearls. When he found one of great value, he went away and sold everything he had and bought it" (Matthew 13:45–46). Same basic idea, just told a little bit differently.

"Wait a minute, Phil," you say. "What does all of this talk about buried treasure have to do with Christmas?"

Hang on, I'm fixing on connecting the dots. You see, when we talk about the kingdom of God, it's about searching and finding something of extraordinary value. It's being willing to give up everything for that gift. You might say these parables are two sides of the same coin: In both stories, Jesus is the priceless gift. When He's found, there needs to be a willingness on our part to give up everything in order to possess the gift of Christ.

Are you with me so far?

On the heels of these parables, something worthy of note happens.

In Matthew 13:53–54, we read: "When Jesus had finished these parables, he moved on from there. Coming to his hometown, he began teaching the people in their synagogue, and they were amazed. 'Where did this man get this wisdom and these miraculous powers?' they asked." So, after delivering five or six powerful parables, Jesus heads back home, where He speaks to the local crowd. They're equally astonished by His teaching and miracles—at least they were at first.

That's when folks recognized Him and began to question His pedigree.

His neighbors said, "Isn't this the carpenter's son? Isn't his mother's name Mary, and aren't his brothers James, Joseph, Simon and Judas? Aren't all his sisters with us? Where then did this man get all these things?" (Matthew 13:55–56). Faster than you can snap your fingers, their amazement took a nasty turn. I mean, they're cutting Him down basically saying things like, "Who cares about this guy? What makes Him so special? Don't we know His family? What's the big deal about Him?" In other words, they were asking, "Why should I care about this guy or His message?"

Look at the next line: "And they took offense at him" (Matthew 13:57a). I like the way one translation puts it: "They got their noses all out of joint" (MSG). One minute He's a miracle worker in their eyes, the next minute that bunch of rascals had no use for Him. Jesus, in turn, said to them: "'A prophet is not without honor except in his own town and in his own home.' And he did not do many miracles there because of their lack of faith" (Matthew 13:57b–58). This got me to thinking…since Jesus was fully God and fully man—complete with the emotions and feelings that you and I have—the words His neighbors hurled at Him *had* to have been hurtful to hear.

Keep in mind it's not a sin to have your feelings hurt.

For thirty years Jesus lived next door to them. These were His friends. Some of them were people whom He worked for as a carpenter. Without a doubt, Jesus handcrafted, built, and sold things to them. They should at least have recognized there was something special about this man. I mean, everything Jesus made displayed perfect craftsmanship. Zero mistakes, right? Jesus was a flawless man, which means He never made a mistake.

He didn't cut corners. He didn't sell second-rate goods.

Instead of praising Him—or at least tipping their hats in His direction—they said, in essence, "What's so special about you?" Noticing how they failed to recognize His divine nature, I got to thinking: If the God of the universe—who created all things, who made a decision to send His only Son to this old dust ball we call earth to become a human being—if the Almighty had looked down from His throne in heaven and seen this moment in time, what if He had said, "If Jesus is going to be mocked, disrespected and treated like that by the human race, I'm not sending my Son down there. It's not worth it"?

I'll tell you what—we'd all be in a heap of trouble if the Almighty had moved on that line of reasoning. Which is why it's instructive to weigh the implications for us if, for whatever reason, Jesus had never been born. You see, if He had chosen not to be born, certain things would not have happened. Of course, the world wouldn't be celebrating Christmas. On a deeper level, there'd be no hope for God's empathy. None.

You see, there's a world of difference between *empathy* and *sympathy*.

Sympathy is to look at someone and to have compassion over their loss, their pain or suffering, or some other personal hardship. You've probably offered sympathy to a friend when their loved one died. But empathy is to be *in* that experience—to know and to have a level of understanding where you see and feel exactly what someone else is seeing and feeling. If Jesus had not come to earth, then we would have no hope for His empathy.

It's an undeniable fact that we needed Jesus to become one of us.

You say, "Why is His becoming one of us so important?"

Jesus was born in that manger two thousand years ago so that He would be made like us *in every way*—I'm talking from cradle to grave, complete with emotions, feelings, and the ability to experience the temptations we all face. Why? In order that He might become a merciful and faithful high priest in service to God as He makes atonement for the sins of the people. Put another way, because He was tempted, Jesus knows from firsthand experience what it's like when we are being tempted. Having been fully human, He now can empathize with our struggles. If Jesus had not become flesh and become one of us, we would not have received this gift of His empathy.

We also wouldn't have had a clear view of God's eternal nature.

The only way we can understand the eternal nature of God is to see Christ and for Him to come and become one of us. He told His disciples, "Anyone who has seen me has seen the Father" (John 14:9). Paul says in Colossians 2:9, "For in Christ all the fullness of the deity lives in bodily form," and the power of the resurrection was there as our glimpse of eternal nature of glory and flesh.

If He had not come to this earth, we would have no clear view of what eternity is really all about.

So, if Jesus had never been born, there would be no hope for any of us. None. In fact, Jesus *had* to come to this earth to show us the way to heaven. If He had never come, then He wouldn't have been able to die on the cross as payment for the sins of the world since there is nothing you or I can do to take away the stain of our sin. Which leads us to the quintessential question…

What if Jesus had never died on the cross?

What if Jesus hadn't walked out of that tomb after three days?

What if He hadn't shown Himself to five hundred witnesses before leaving this world to go back to the Father? Answer: I would have no representation in heaven. I would have no one there who really understands what humanity is all about. I would have no one standing at the right hand of God saying that I am one of His children. And yet Jesus is there in heaven today mediating for you and me.

Here's our dilemma. Every one of us winds up in a six-foot hole in the ground with no way out. Jesus came to earth to be available to die on that cross and rise from the dead to give you and me hope of life eternal. Which is why I said at the outset that Christmas is my favorite time of year. I no longer have to fear death. Nor do you—that is, if you confess your need for a Savior, repent from your sin, and put your faith in Jesus.

What if you do that? You'll be eternally good to go!

*Glory to God in the
highest heaven, and on
earth peace to those on
whom his favor rests.*

LUKE 2:14

———————————

4

The Second Sunday of Advent

WALK A MILE IN MARY'S SANDALS

Courtesy Phil and Miss Kay Robertson

Read Micah 5:2–4

"'But you, Bethlehem Ephrathah, though you are small among the clans of Judah, out of you will come for me one who will be ruler over Israel, whose origins are from of old, from ancient times.' Therefore Israel will be abandoned until the time when she who is in labor bears a son, and the rest of his brothers return to join the Israelites. He will stand and shepherd his flock in the strength of the Lord, in the majesty of the name of the Lord his God. And they will live securely, for then his greatness will reach to the ends of the earth."

One of the most popular *Duck Dynasty* episodes was when Phil and I finally got the wedding we never had. I'm a patient woman. I mean, it took almost fifty years for that event! Our yard had been transformed into a wedding chapel of sorts. And, with four generations of Robertsons gathered around us, we renewed our vows. My heart almost couldn't contain the joy I felt standing there next to Phil as our son Alan officiated the ceremony. There's nothing more beautiful than a bride filled with hopes and dreams on her wedding day.

Two thousand years ago, Mary, a young virgin, was betrothed to her man. I'm sure she was dreaming of the life they would share together. Joseph was a lot like Phil— a good, hardworking man. Mary must have known that

Joseph, skilled as a carpenter, would be a wonderful provider. My hunch is that she even had plans for him to build her a kitchen table as the centerpiece of their new home together.

That's when the Angel Gabriel delivered some earth-shaking news—she was going to have a child. Gabriel said, "You will conceive and give birth to a son, and you are to call him Jesus. He will be great and will be called the Son of the Most High. The Lord God will give him the throne of his father David, and he will reign over Jacob's descendants forever; his kingdom will never end" (Luke 1:31–33).

One of the things I love about Mary is that she was a practical woman. She wanted the specifics of how this would work. That's how I am. When Phil or one of the boys announces one of their big ideas, I want to know how they plan to pull it off. In Mary's case, she asked the angel, "How will this be…since I am a virgin?" (Luke 1:34). Even though Gabriel briefed her on the details, on some level Mary had to be a bit frightened by the implications of this heavenly headline. You know, "Would everyone around town think less of me because I'm pregnant out of wedlock?"

I'm sure she wondered how the news would impact her life, her dreams, her plans—and her future with Joseph in her community. Unlike today, unwed pregnant mothers weren't looked upon too kindly back then. They were often shunned or even disowned as a disgrace to their families. Not to mention that by most estimates Nazareth was a small backwater town—way smaller than West Monroe, Louisiana, where we live. I'm talking there were maybe less than a thousand people.

Trust me, gossip travels faster in small towns than a dog with his tail on fire. In spite of her fears of what her neighbors or family might think, Mary submitted to the will of God. She embraced her role as the vessel that God would use to bring His Son into the world. Through her baby, brought about by the power of the Holy Spirit, God promised to bring salvation.

I'm sure you're familiar with how the story unfolded— nine months later Jesus was born in a manger surrounded by cattle. I'm fascinated with what Mary must have felt holding this baby in her arms. She had to wonder about His destiny. Having been raised in a Jewish home, a descendant of the mighty King David, and knowing that her child was the Promised One that the prophet Micah spoke about in today's text, Mary knew God had placed a special calling on His life.

Jesus would be the redemption of mankind.

If Mary was anything like me, even as she was weaning her baby, I bet she was trying to picture the day when He would be old enough to do what God had called Him to do. That's what we mommas do, right? We get to thinking about their choice of friends, where they'll go to college, who they'll marry—all while they're still in diapers. I'm sure Mary spent some time envisioning the life Jesus would live. Like any other Jewish boy, He would work hard with His hands learning the family trade alongside of His father. She probably had the confidence that He would love and respect them as parents.

We're not told much about the period of His life as He grew into a young boy.

I'd love to know more about those years, wouldn't you?

Yet, it's just a mystery. From the time He was twelve years old until He showed up to start His earthly ministry, we don't have any other details. We can only assume He was as normal as a person could be—while also being the sinless Son of God. As Mary watched Jesus grow into a man, she must have had some apprehension—I'm talking about once He began to do miracles and draw huge crowds. Did you know there were times when He had so many people following Him, hanging on to every word, that Mary and her family couldn't even get close to Him?

Jesus's disciple Luke wrote about one such occasion: "Now Jesus' mother and brothers came to see him, but they were not able to get near him because of the crowd" (Luke 8:19). Phil and I have seen our share of massive crowds when we've traveled and spoken around the world. Those can be exciting times because we felt like this was our calling from God. Likewise, Mary must have realized that this ministry of Jesus's was the destiny that the angel had told her about all those years earlier.

At the same time, she knew there was a growing throng of enemies. There were those among the Jewish leadership who began to murmur about the threat that His life represented to their grip on power and authority in the community. They constantly plotted to "trap" Jesus into saying something that they could use against Him to silence Him. There was ultimately talk of His death.

Surely Mary didn't fully understand all of that. Why would anyone reject Jesus? All she ever saw Him do was heal people who were blind, deaf, crippled, paralyzed, and demon possessed, and forgive adulterers, tax collectors, and sinners of all stripes. What's not to love about that? Plus, Gabriel had said Jesus would be "called the Son of God" (Luke 1:35b). Why, then, would people be gunning for Him?

Then, of course, there was that fateful day when she learned that her son had been betrayed by one of His closest friends—the Disciple Judas—who turned Him over to be crucified. I cannot fathom what Mary felt when Pilate washed his hands and turned Him over to be whipped beyond recognition. Watching her son drag the cross through the city streets of Jerusalem and then be nailed to it and displayed for the world to see on the hill called Calvary, that must have crushed her heart.

I wouldn't have faulted her one bit if she struggled to accept that all of this was a necessary part of His destiny. If I'm her, I'm thinking, "Didn't Gabriel say I was highly favored? Didn't he say the Lord was with me? If I'm so favored, why must they kill my son? Why must He suffer like that?" After an agonizing day of torture, ridicule, and shame, Mary's boy breathed His last.

I'm sure all of His followers, including Mary, wept bitter tears. Those who loved Him, those who were fed by His hand when He took a few loaves and fish to feed a multitude, and those who were healed by a touch of His hands must have been totally confused by the finality of His death. If I had been in Mary's sandals, I would have wondered, "What does all of this mean? Three years of teaching and healing and now He's dead? Is that it?"

In the midst of the widespread uncertainty, fear, and despair among His disciples, an amazing thing occurred three days later. On a bright Sunday morning, a rumor circulated: Jesus wasn't in the tomb where they had put His body. Mary must have wondered, "Could it be true? Did someone take His body?" That's when more unbelievable news surfaced: several people claimed to have walked and talked with Him (Luke 24:31–34). If true, her son had not stayed dead but had come back to life! But, how could that be…unless…Jesus was not just her son, but the risen, living, breathing Son of God.

Maybe that was the moment she finally both *understood* and *believed* what He and the angel had said about His destiny. I'm sure she recalled the Sabbath when Jesus stood up in the synagogue and, reading from Isaiah 61:1–2, said, "The Spirit of the Lord is on me, because he has anointed me to proclaim good news to the poor. He has sent me to proclaim freedom for the prisoners and recovery of sight for the blind, to set the oppressed free." That's when He went on to make the startling claim: "Today this scripture is fulfilled in your hearing" (Luke 4:21b).

There's no way Mary would have forgotten that moment. How could she?

His statement literally caused a riot!

Luke writes, "All the people in the synagogue were furious when they heard this. They got up, drove him out of town, and took him to the brow of the hill on which the town was built, in order to throw him off the cliff. But he walked right through the crowd and went on his way" (Luke 4:28–30). They were seething mad because Jesus declared He had been sent by God to set them free.

Jesus had made other startling claims—like the time He said, "I am the way and the truth and the life. No one comes to the Father except through me" (John 14:6). He told His disciples that He would die and come back to life (Mark 8:31). He even spoke about the day when He would return to earth and take all those who believed in Him home to be with His Father in heaven (Matthew 24:30–31).

There's no way around it. This child born in Bethlehem, Jesus of Nazareth, has forever impacted all of eternity! Without hesitation, Phil and I would give our very lives for this Man. That wasn't always the case. As Phil has said many times, he was an angry, commode-hugging, mean old drunk for years before he ran up on Jesus. And I had my share of wayward ways, too. That all changed when we stopped looking at the baby Jesus and placed our faith in the risen Jesus.

How about you?

Are you experiencing the joy of Jesus this Christmas?

She will give birth to a son, and you are to give him the name Jesus, because he will save his people from their sins.

MATTHEW 1:21

_____

5

The Third Sunday
of Advent

THE BABY CHANGES EVERYTHING

Courtesy Phil and Miss Kay Robertson

"In those days John the Baptist came, preaching in the wilderness of Judea and saying, 'Repent, for the kingdom of heaven has come near.' This is he who was spoken of through the prophet Isaiah: 'A voice of one calling in the wilderness, "Prepare the way for the Lord, make straight paths for him."'"

When Alan, Willie, Jep, and Jase were young, they didn't take to putting on a little Christmas skit in the living room the way kids do. It's funny that my boys never did that for us. You've got to understand that Phil, when he was a boy, wasn't one who did that sort of thing, either. He was all about cutting down a tree for Christmas and hunting or fishing for the Christmas dinner. So I'm not entirely surprised my kids didn't put on a Christmas play in our home.

Thankfully, my grandbabies like dressing up and playing the various people in the Christmas story. They'll get up in front of the fireplace like it's their stage to sing the carols and perform the skits they've worked up. Sometimes Reed will get his guitar so he and Cole will get to singing with the others. That's a real highlight—although sometimes, since I'm the grandmamma, they want me to perform with them.

You'd think by now they'd know I can't sing a lick.

But I do give Alan credit. Back when he was pastoring our church during the 1990s, he made up for lost time. Year after year he arranged a full-on Christmas musical production at the church. Mind you, not all those Christmas dramas were about the birth of Christ. In other words, sometimes he'd take a bit of "creative license." He'd expand them with snapshots of events from the Old Testament that foreshadowed the coming of the Messiah. I thought that was a pretty cool deal.

One year Alan had a giant, semitransparent screen set up on stage, and they acted out a variety of scenes from Adam and Eve forward, silhouetted behind the screen. He wanted to make the connection to the reason why Jesus had to come to earth in the first place, going all the way back to the Garden of Eden, where Adam and Eve sinned and broke our relationship with God. That's the bad news. The good news is that God prepared a way for us to restore our fellowship with Him when He promised to send us a Savior. Alan wanted the Christmas drama that year to be an evangelistic outreach of sorts. I'd say he did a great job.

I can remember the year that we did the Nativity scene. Willie and Korie played Joseph and Mary, and John Luke was baby Jesus in the manger. All of us played different roles. Some of us were peasants or the shepherds or whatever. The whole family got into the act. But I'll never forget the year that Phil played the part of John the Baptist. Talk about typecasting! That story is a bit unusual since technically speaking Jesus's cousin John the Baptist wasn't part of the manger scene.

Like I said, Alan would feature different stories from the Bible related to the reason and significance of Christmas. Well, Phil carried a big staff about as tall as he is and got all dressed up in animal skins. I don't remember if they were real animal skins, but I wouldn't be surprised if they had been genuine deer pelts or something. After all, the Bible says, "John's clothes were made of camel's hair, and he had a leather belt around his waist. His food was locusts and wild honey" (Matthew 3:4).

I've always pictured John the Baptist as being a bit rough around the edges—but, hey, so are we Robertsons. Phil really got into his part. He even memorized all of his lines. That night, standing at the back of the church, Phil pounded his staff on the floor so hard that the place shook. As he started to walk slowly down the center aisle, he shouted, "Repent! For the kingdom of heaven has come near!" Believe me, he really *screamed* his lines. He didn't need a microphone. I mean, he was John the Baptist pointing the way to Christ and wanted everyone in shouting distance to know. The way Phil's voice boomed from the back of the auditorium all the way to the front was, oh my goodness, just amazing!

Well, at least I thought so.

But the kids in the auditorium—they were a different story. They started crying and literally took cover by hiding under the pews! It scared them so bad. We did three performances—a Friday, Saturday, and Sunday in early December—and he'd scare the daylights out of the kids every time. That's the truth. In a way, the speech that John the Baptist originally gave scared the daylights out of the people who heard him proclaim it, too, although for different reasons. His message *was* harsh, especially toward the Pharisees and Sadducees—the religious leaders in the temple at the time.

Here's what John said in Matthew 3:7b–10: "You brood of vipers! Who warned you to flee from the coming wrath?" How's that for an opening line? I can imagine the look on the collective faces of the Pharisees and Sadducees—let's just say they weren't accustomed to being called out or put under conviction. He continued: "Produce fruit in keeping with repentance." In other words, John was pointing out that from God's view it wasn't good enough to walk around in flowing robes spouting spiritual platitudes while bragging (as they often did) about how they kept the letter of the law. Instead, God desired a repentant heart.

John the Baptist was just warming up.

As if he had read their minds, John said, "And do not think you can say to yourselves, 'We have Abraham as our father.' I tell you that out of these stones God can raise up children for Abraham." You see, the religious leaders were quick to point out their heritage as if that somehow made them acceptable in the sight of the Almighty. Unlike many in the crowd who were readily "confessing their sins" and were "baptized by him in the Jordan River" (Matthew 3:6), the Pharisees and Sadducees thought they were above all of that. They figured that they were good to go with God because of their self-righteousness and piety.

They figured wrong.

Since John wasn't one to mince words, he boldly warned them: "The ax is already at the root of the trees, and every tree that does not produce good fruit will be cut down and thrown into the fire" (Matthew 3:10). As jarring as that message was, John was doing them—and us—a favor by giving us a heads-up regarding the true nature of the Messiah. According to the prophet Isaiah, John came to "prepare the way for the Lord." Those preparations included explaining that all of us need to repent from sin and then use our lives to "produce good fruit."

The way I see it, during the Christmas season we can get all warm and fuzzy over the notion of baby Jesus sleeping in the manger...with the star perched overhead...and the cattle gently swaying as if they had practiced their choreography for months before His birth. I'm as sentimental as the next person. And there's nothing wrong with delighting in these pictures of that first Christmas. But the fact of the matter is that Jesus was born to free us from the bondage of sin and death. That's serious business, y'all. His birth changed everything.

Since some of us will respond in faith, repent, and be baptized into new life in Jesus while others will reject Him, there's bound to be a division—even within the same family. Jesus Himself said, "Do not suppose that I have come to bring peace to the earth. I did not come to bring peace, but a sword" (Matthew 10:34). In other words, the Messiah would separate believers from unbelievers. John put it this way: "His winnowing fork is in his hand, and he will clear his threshing floor, gathering his wheat into the barn and burning up the chaff with unquenchable fire" (Matthew 3:12).

None of us have an excuse. We've been forewarned. We can embrace the love and grace of Jesus and be saved, or we can reject Him—as the religious leaders did back then—and be cast away from His presence for all of eternity. Let's not get so caught up in the gift giving, the yummy food, and the merriment of Christmas and miss what's really going on here.

In Matthew 13:47–48, this Christ Child whose birth we celebrate is now a grown man. Here, Jesus told a parable that makes my point. He said, "Once again, the kingdom of heaven is like a net that was let down into the lake and caught all kinds of fish. When it was full, the fishermen pulled it up on the shore. Then they sat down and collected the good fish in baskets, but threw the bad away."

You know, I come from a fishing family so I can appreciate what this parable is all about. Phil and the boys call them "trash fish." They'll haul in their nets from the river down by our house and sort out the fish. It's really sad for those discarded fish because they were just what they were—useless trash. Until the boys learned the ropes, Phil was the one who deemed them trash. He knew from experience which fish people wouldn't eat. If the fish were uneatable, then the fish market wouldn't buy them. If they wouldn't buy those fish, then we couldn't make any money—and that's why we were out there fishing in the first place.

So, I get this picture about the kingdom of God being like a net. There's trash fish and there's good fish all tangled up in there, and they need to be sorted out. Looking back at the text, Jesus explains, "This is how it will be at the end of the age. The angels will come and separate the wicked from the righteous and throw them into the blazing furnace, where there will be weeping and gnashing of teeth" (Matthew 13:49–50). That, my friend, is a picture of hell—where none of us want to be.

You see, He's much more than a sweet little baby in a manger—He's our promised, all-powerful Messiah. Whether you watch your kids or grandkids reenact the Christmas story by the fireplace or you attend a full-blown Christmas musical at church, don't lose sight of the fact that Jesus came to rescue you and me from hell. He may have come the first time as a baby—but when He returns, He'll be coming in a "blazing fire with his powerful angels. He will punish those who do not know God and do not obey the gospel of our Lord Jesus" (2 Thessalonians 1:7b–8).

This Christmas is the perfect time to answer: Are you ready for His return?

The Word became flesh and made his dwelling among us. We have seen his glory, the glory of the one and only Son, who came from the Father, full of grace and truth.

JOHN 1:14

6

The Fourth Sunday of Advent

THE PLACE, PEOPLE, AND PURPOSE
OF CHRISTMAS

"For God did not send his Son into the world to condemn the world, but to save the world through him.... The thief comes only to steal and kill and destroy; I have come that they may have life, and have it to the full."

When Miss Kay and I renewed our vows on an episode of *Duck Dynasty*, my brother Si was given the task of distracting us. Hey, he knows a thing or two about being distracted at work, so they figured he'd be the right one to distract us. His job was to keep us away from home long enough for the others to set up for the outdoor ceremony. I mean to tell you, old Si drove us all over creation to certain places that were supposedly significant to us. I told him, "It would be nice if you went down memory lane to run up on something that you actually remembered." Si finally took us to a tree where Miss Kay and I had carved our initials in it almost fifty years ago.

There's something meaningful about reflecting on the important places in life.

For example, our oldest son, Alan, was born on January 5, 1965. When he came forth from Miss Kay's loins into the world, Alan made a real splash. Why? Because he was the first baby birthed in Lincoln Parish, Louisiana, that year. I mean to tell you, his arrival on the scene was a big media event. There was even a photographer who swung by to take a picture of us. *Tens* of people were there to celebrate the moment. Okay, while nobody arranged a parade to commemorate that happy, happy, happy occasion, the place where he was born has special meaning to us.

From the moment he took his first breath, Alan's life has profoundly impacted Miss Kay and me for the better. Everything wasn't always rosy with our firstborn son, mind you. There were a number of times when I needed to invoke the "Robertson Code" whereby I applied three licks of my belt to the seat of Alan's understanding when he disrespected Miss Kay, busted up perfectly fine equipment, or engaged in a fight wherein blows or kicks were exchanged.

But once Alan was finished with his tomfoolery stage, he went on to become a pastor. His ministry has touched the lives of countless people here in West Monroe, Louisiana, and literally around the world wherever he's traveled to spread the Good News of Jesus. Alan will jump on a plane at the drop of a hat to preach the Word. That's because he understands the Almighty has placed a purpose, a calling on his life.

That got me to thinking about the birth of Jesus. I'd like to briefly look at His life from three different perspectives: the significance of the *place* where He was born, the *people* His birth touched, and the *purpose* He gives us—just like I illustrated with Alan's life a moment ago.

Regarding the significance of the "place" where Jesus was born, Bethlehem was one of the smaller towns in Israel. But there was something unique about it. The Apostle Luke writes, "In those days Caesar Augustus issued a decree that a census should be taken of the entire Roman world.... And everyone went to their own town to register. So Joseph also went up from the town of Nazareth in Galilee to Judea, to Bethlehem the town of David, because he belonged to the house and line of David" (Luke 2:1–4).

You see, God left nothing to chance. Joseph was from the line of David. This ensured they would wind up in the right place—Bethlehem—at the right time to bring forth God's Son into this world. Luke records that Joseph "went there to register with Mary, who was pledged to be married to him and was expecting a child. While they were there, the time came for the baby to be born, and she gave birth to her firstborn, a son. She wrapped him in cloths and placed him in a manger, because there was no guest room available for them" (Luke 2:5–7).

Bethlehem was the stomping grounds for a lot of biblical history. For example, Rachel, who was the mother of the Twelve Tribes, was buried there (Genesis 48:7). This was also the place where Ruth met and married Boaz. The whole story of Ruth took place in the town of Bethlehem (see Ruth 1). And, the place where Jesus was born was the same place where David, a shepherd, was secretly anointed king of Israel by the prophet Samuel (1 Samuel 16).

There's more. The name "Bethlehem" literally means "house of bread." You say, "Phil, why is that important?" I contend it's not a coincidence that the "house of bread" would also be the birthplace of Jesus. Think about it. He said of Himself, "I am the bread of life" (John 6:35). Elsewhere, Jesus said, "I am the living bread that came down from heaven. Whoever eats this bread will live forever. This bread is my flesh, which I will give for the life of the world" (John 6:51). Did you catch it? Three times in one verse Jesus uses the bread metaphor to describe Himself.

Are you beginning to see the picture? The Almighty had a plan all along to bring the Messiah into the world through this seed line of David (Luke 3:21–38). He wanted the Jews to understand that this really was the promised Messiah, the Bread of Life. Bethlehem was a very special place to God, rich with biblical significance—not just some random town Joseph and Mary showed up in because Caesar Augustus issued a decree.

Let's move from the significance of the "place" where Jesus was born to the "people" His birth touched. For starters, when the angels were sent from the throne room of God, who did they break the glorious news to? Was it King Herod? Or Caesar Augustus, the ruler of the known world back then? Was it the elite? Or the highly educated ruling Jewish council? Nope.

He chose the shepherds—a rag-tag group of men "keeping watch over their flocks at night" just outside of Bethlehem. I say that because these dudes were actually "living out in the fields" (Luke 2:8). I know a thing or two about living out in the wild for extended periods of time without the comforts or amenities of home. Think about it. There'd be no bathrooms. No showers. No beds. Just lots of nasty dust and dirt clinging to your whiskers, hair, sandals, and clothes from sleeping on the ground and following the southbound end of a northbound sheep.

Living like that for days on end is enough to drive a fellow a tad crazy.

No doubt they looked rougher than me—and smelled bad, too. What's more, during that period in history, shepherds were considered with the same low regard as Gypsies or vagrants. Most were uneducated, illiterate, and untrusted. Did you know that shepherds were not allowed to testify in a court of law? You say, "Why?" Because their testimony simply wasn't trustworthy.

In spite of their subpar reputation, God chose them to reveal the greatest news humankind would ever receive. I think it's pretty cool that thousands of years before the events of this night transpired, David had been a shepherd tending his flocks in the same area, unaware that the night sky he saw would one day be teeming with angels.

While the shepherds were working the night shift, "an angel of the Lord appeared to them, and the glory of the Lord shone around them, and they were terrified. But the angel said to them, 'Do not be afraid. I bring you good news that will cause great joy for all the people. Today in the town of David a Savior has been born to you; he is the Messiah, the Lord. This will be a sign to you: You will find a baby wrapped in cloths and lying in a manger'" (Luke 2:9–12).

Two things worthy of note here. First, the angel said this news was for "all the people"—that would include them. As if that wasn't clear enough, the angel said "a Savior has been born to you." Tell me that's not incredible news! Regardless of your standing on earth, Jesus came to save us. Doesn't matter if your reputation isn't worth a hoot. Doesn't matter if you don't have a formal education, you don't own property, or you live like a homeless Gypsy. The Almighty made it clear from the get-go that He is not a respecter of persons. Years later, the Apostle Peter came to that same conclusion when he said, "I now realize how true it is that God does not show favoritism" (Acts 10:34).

The shepherds "hurried off" to play their part in this world-changing event. They had been deputized by an angel, sent from heaven itself, to find Joseph and Mary and the baby Jesus and to report what they had seen and heard. In other words, the "people" His birth touched included the down-and-outers, proving the point that the Almighty came for everyone and He can and does use *anybody* to advance His kingdom.

That's mighty good news for a fellow like me—a man who, for the first twenty-eight years of my life, was heading in the wrong direction. Just like the shepherds of old, when I gave my heart to Jesus, I received from Him a high calling and a fresh purpose. Notice how the shepherds were impacted. Luke writes, "The shepherds returned, glorifying and praising God for all the things they had heard and seen, which were just as they had been told" (Luke 2:20). No question, their lives were forever changed.

That's the power of Christianity. Once we give our hearts to Jesus, we have a new "purpose," namely, to serve and to tell others about the life-changing power of the Christ Child. You might say that Jesus came here with an upside-down view of leadership. He said that "the Son of Man did not come to be served, but to serve, and to give his life as a ransom for many" (Matthew 20:28). Jesus came to this earth, and became a human being, to serve us, to love us, and to die for us so one day we can live with Him in all of His glory in heaven.

Remember that Jesus's first birth is what makes our second birth possible. Both of those are demonstrations of God's grace. That's why they call it amazing. On this fourth Sunday of Advent, why not reflect on the place, the people, and the purpose of those who were part of that first Christmas? As you do, keep in mind that you, too, are a part of the story. The birth happened so that you could be a part of God's family. You have a new purpose—to live for Him and to share His story with other people.

Look, the food will be eaten up. The decorations will be taken down. Your guests will leave. The house will be quiet once again. The fact of the matter is this: if Christmas is only an annual celebration with lots of hullabaloo, you'll be left with little more than an empty feeling in your heart. What's the good news? When Christ fills your heart, friends and family can leave, decorations can be stored in the attic, but your life will remain full of joy and peace and glad tidings. Jesus came that you may have life and have it to its fullest. That's what Miss Kay and I want you to have.

We want you to have an abundant life in Jesus.

The Birth of Jesus

In those days Caesar Augustus issued a decree that a census should be taken of the entire Roman world. (This was the first census that took place while Quirinius was governor of Syria.) And everyone went to their own town to register.

So Joseph also went up from the town of Nazareth in Galilee to Judea, to Bethlehem the town of David, because he belonged to the house and line of David. He went there to register with Mary, who was pledged to be married to him and was expecting a child. While they were there, the time came for the baby to be born, and she gave birth to her firstborn, a son. She wrapped him in cloths and placed him in a manger, because there was no guest room available for them.

And there were shepherds living out in the fields nearby, keeping watch over their flocks at night. An angel of the Lord appeared to them, and the glory of the Lord shone around them, and they were terrified. But the angel said to them, "Do not be afraid. I bring you good news that will cause great joy for all the people. Today in the town of David a Savior has been born to you; he is the Messiah, the Lord. This will be a sign to you: You will find a baby wrapped in cloths and lying in a manger."

Suddenly a great company of the heavenly host appeared with the angel, praising God and saying,

"Glory to God in the highest heaven, and on earth peace to those on whom his favor rests."

When the angels had left them and gone into heaven, the shepherds said to one another, "Let's go to Bethlehem and see this thing that has happened, which the Lord has told us about."

So they hurried off and found Mary and Joseph, and the baby, who was lying in the manger. When they had seen him, they spread the word concerning what had been told them about this child, and all who heard it were amazed at what the shepherds said to them. But Mary treasured up all these things and pondered them in her heart. The shepherds returned, glorifying and praising God for all the things they had heard and seen, which were just as they had been told.

LUKE 2

7

The Robertsons' Top Ten Favorite Christmas Movies

I confess I am a die-hard Christmas movie fan. I mean to tell you, when the Hallmark Channel starts playing its Christmas movies, I'm there. I mean, I'm watching its Christmas movies all the way from November through December. They're such good, clean movies. From *It's a Wonderful Life* and *A Christmas Carol*, to both versions of *Miracle on 34th Street*, I'm hooked.

When Al, Willie, Jase, and Jep were little, they absolutely loved to watch animated Christmas movies on the TV. Of course, we were too poor to afford going to the theater, so the kids just camped out in front of the television to watch *A Charlie Brown Christmas*, *Frosty the Snowman*, and *Dr. Seuss' How the Grinch Stole Christmas!*

As the boys grew older, hands down our all-time favorite was *Christmas Vacation*, which we just can't miss. We mainly love it because of the whacky family antics. Those crazy aunts and uncles hit close to home with the Robertsons. And we never grow tired of *A Christmas Story*. As a momma of four rifle-toting rascals, I liked all of the gun safety they learned growing up in that movie— like never aiming at others and only drawing down on what you intended on shooting, whether it was a BB gun or a 30-30 rifle. And, since we always had a lot of stray dogs running around, the scene where the dogs knock down the Christmas turkey was hilarious. It reminds me of the time when our strays got into our cook shack and broke Phil's favorite fish-cooking pot.

Now that the boys have families of their own, I love it when my grandbabies discover something I watched as a child. Last Christmas I watched the Claymation version of *Rudolph the Red-Nosed Reindeer* with them. They were captivated by it and adored it. Even though that film was made fifty years ago and was definitely "low tech," there was still something magical about the message.

That got Phil and me thinking that it'd be a fun idea to list ten of our favorite Christmas movies along with a few questions to discuss with your family and friends. We've even identified a key theme to look for as you watch. Now, if you'll excuse me, I think I'll pour a cup of Phil's Famous Hot Cocoa (see page 119) and settle in for a Christmas movie marathon!

—Miss Kay

IT'S A WONDERFUL LIFE (1946)

STARRING: James Stewart, Donna Reed
THEME: Servanthood

It's a Wonderful Life isn't just one of our favorite Christmas movies, it's one of our favorite films of all time! It doesn't matter how many times I've seen it, the story of George and Mary Bailey, Clarence the angel, the evil Mr. Potter, and the other residents of Bedford Falls pulls me in every time. It seems with each passing year our world gets more and more like Potterville, doesn't it? But the innocence of Bedford Falls is available to us if we're willing to work as hard as George to make it a better place.

Oh, how I want to have George Bailey's heart all year long. He was smart as a tack but also a wide-eyed dreamer and romantic who spent his life serving others. He didn't hesitate to rush into harm's way to save his brother or to stay behind to help his father run the family business. He set aside his own adventures—and even his own honeymoon—to save his neighbors from Mr. Potter. George's life was spent serving everyone but himself. In the end, sweet old Clarence gets to show him just how special the gift of life and a life of service really is.

Phil and I can't imagine what the world would be like without this beautiful story.

1. In John 15:13 Jesus says, "Greater love has no one than this: to lay down one's life for one's friends." What are some ways that others have laid their lives down for you?

2. Can you think of one or two things that would be significantly different in your life if any of the people in the room with you right now had never been born?

3. In Matthew 6 Jesus has a lot to say about helping the needy, how to pray, how to truly store up treasures, and how to handle stress and worry in the light of God's goodness. How many specific lines in this chapter of the Bible remind you of George Bailey and his actions?

MIRACLE ON 34TH STREET (1947)

STARRING: Maureen O'Hara, John Payne, Natalie Wood
THEME: Faith

C hristmas is about Jesus and not Santa Claus, but few movies reinforce the importance of faith the way *Miracle on 34th Street* does. Besides, did you know that the name Kris Kringle is based on the name *Christkindl*—which is German for Christ Child? No matter what people try to add or take away from Christmas, this season has always been, and will always be, about Jesus.

The aspect I love most about *Miracle* is that everyone is forced to make a decision about Kris. All of those sophisticated New York professionals living in Yuppieville have to deal with this lovely old man who exudes grace, mercy, and love to everyone he meets. The children understand right away. Kris knows how to listen to them, how to speak to them, and how to provide exactly what they need. Jesus said that unless we change and become like children, we will never see the kingdom of heaven. The good news is that He can make us like little kids again!

I absolutely love the last scene, the one with Kris's cane leaning up against the house. I pray that I always have eyes to see the little signs all around me that point to the fact that Jesus is there watching out for me.

1. In Matthew 18:1–5 Jesus turned Jewish society and human instinct on their heads by saying that in order

to see His kingdom, His disciples would have to become like little children again. What qualities do you think Jesus was speaking about when He said that?

2. Think about your own faith story. Are there any ways you would like to become more childlike in your relationship with the Almighty?

3. Right after Jesus cleared the temple of those who had made a mockery of religion by taking advantage of the poor, a group of children shouted, "Hosanna to the Son of David" to Jesus. The chief priests and teachers of the law were offended. But Jesus quoted Psalm 8:2 back at them. Why do you suppose that particular response would be so upsetting to the religious elite?

DR. SEUSS' HOW THE GRINCH STOLE CHRISTMAS! (1966)

STARRING: Boris Karloff, Thurl Ravenscroft
THEME: Redemption

Everything about *Dr. Seuss' How the Grinch Stole Christmas!* was perfect for me as a kid—and still is as an adult. The offbeat humor, the wonderfully odd music, the colorful animation by Chuck Jones (director of the animated classic *Merrie Melodies* and *Looney Tunes* cartoons), and the voice of Boris Karloff all worked together to create a story that was super fun even as it taught us some important truths. The Christmas season can, if we're not careful, bring out the worst parts of our nature. Can I get a witness?!

At the center of this fantastic story is a character so bitter, so angry, and so nasty that he seems beyond all hope. Seuss does such a thorough job of making the Grinch despicable that his ultimate redemption is a complete thrill. It still gets to me every time.

I bet you, like me, know people who we hope will someday have their hearts grow three sizes. Sometimes, though, if I'm completely honest, that Grinch is me! Sure, maybe I don't sneak into town and steal everyone's gifts and food and Christmas trees. But sometimes I can be a bit of a Grinch in my own ways. This wonderful story underlines the fact that none of us are beyond redemption.

Oh, and you'd better believe me when I say we Robertsons love ourselves some roast beast!

1. Romans 2:4 reminds us that it is God's kindness that leads us to repentance. After the Grinch does his best to destroy Christmas, he hears the sounds of the wonderful little Whos singing a song of thankfulness and love. It was that gratefulness and love that caused the Grinch to think that maybe there was more to Christmas than the stuff he had taken. Has God's kindness ever led you to repentance? How?

2. In Colossians 1:13, Paul, a follower of Jesus, reminds us that Jesus is the One who delivers us from darkness by forgiving us of our sins and who, in turn, makes a way for us to enter His heavenly kingdom. Have you been transformed from a Grinch-like villain into a lover of the Light? If not yet, why not make this Christmas the time when you embrace the love Jesus has for you?

3. What are your Grinch-triggers at Christmastime? Which events or experiences take you out of "celebration mode" and into selfish, sinful behaviors? What might you do to prevent those negative distractions in the future?

A CHRISTMAS CAROL (1951)

STARRING: Alastair Sim, Mervyn Johns, Michael Hordern
THEME: Repentance

I'm so glad Charles Dickens chose the romance and grit of an old English Christmas as the background for his fabulous novella *A Christmas Carol*. It is absolutely one of the most redemptive stories of repentance ever written. As far as fantasy stories go, it sure packs an emotional and spiritual punch.

I love the Victorian imagery and the classical flourishes of Dickens' nineteenth-century London. But what I appreciate most about the story of Ebenezer Scrooge is the reminder that it's never too late to have a change of heart this side of eternity. Scrooge's repentance and renewal bolsters my hope in Jesus as the One who makes all things new. Hey, I'm talking even a miserly accountant consumed by greed, resentment, and self-reliance.

And what better time of year for a life-changing repentance than Christmas! Think about it. This holiday honors one of the most important events in all of human history. God's Son left the glories of heaven to be with us in our darkness and to transform it into glorious light. How incredible!

In my book, it's not quite Christmas until we've seen the repentance of Ebenezer Scrooge one more time. This timeless story reminds me of the things that matter most, that life is short, and that none of us know when our final accounting will come. It also reminds me that many of God's blessings show up through tiny, broken people.

1. Read 2 Corinthians 12:10. Tiny Tim may have been physically frail, but Scrooge, the wealthiest man in town, was the sick one. Scrooge needed to be reminded of his past, exposed to the present he was hiding from, and warned about his future in order to change. We Robertsons can certainly relate to that kind of transformation. Who do you identify most with in this movie?

2. A strong secondary theme of caring for the poor resonates throughout *A Christmas Carol.* Although the book was written well over a hundred years ago in England, most of the same challenges remain in place. What do you do at Christmastime to relieve suffering? How about year-round?

3. Scrooge was an accountant, but he counted all the wrong things. In this fantasy story he gets a warning. However, you and I never know when we will be called to make an account for our lives. If you ask God to reveal your sins to you, and to change your heart, He will. After all, we have access to the Holy Spirit, so we don't need ghosts.

A CHARLIE BROWN CHRISTMAS
(1965)

STARRING: Ann Altieri, Chris Doran, Sally Dryer

THEME: Community

Poor Charlie Brown. He's so sincere and yet, far too often, things don't work out for him. After Snoopy's house-decorating competition and Sally's letter to Santa, the last straw for Charlie Brown was when Lucy sent him to get a "shiny aluminum" tree for the play. That he could only find a measly sapling only added to his frustration and dismay. Little did Charlie Brown know what his group of friends could accomplish with a humble shrub and a bit of faith!

Beneath the surface of this anti-commercialism tale is a subtle reflection on the power of friends and family to shape us. Charlie Brown's heart just wasn't ready for Christmas yet. Then Linus steps up. I don't know if I've ever heard a more powerful reading of Luke 2:8–14 than the one he unloads on Charlie at the climax of the story.

It was the power of community, sparked by a fresh reminder of the true meaning of Christmas, that turned Charlie Brown's pathetic sapling into a beautiful Christmas tree. You may not always feel joyful at Christmastime. But if you surround yourself with other believers and reread the story of the incarnation, it's hard to stay grumpy. Our hearts, like Charlie Brown's tree, just need a little care sometimes.

1. Read Luke 2:8–14. Why do you think it is so easy to lose the point of Christmas the way a child might lose a treasure in a pile of ripped wrapping paper? Which trappings of the season distract you from the main point?

2. Shepherds are a tight-knit culture. How do you imagine the birth of Christ impacted their community in the weeks, months, and years following that amazing night when the angels told them of His birth?

3. Whether related to Christmas or not, can you think of a time when your friends or loved ones came to your rescue? Or a time when you came to the aid of a friend?

FROSTY THE SNOWMAN (1969)

STARRING: Jackie Vernon, Billy De Wolfe, Jimmy Durante
THEME: Rebirth

*F*rosty the Snowman immediately transports me back to my childhood. I remember the original song by Gene Autry, the Little Golden Book, and then the amazing animated TV special from the late 1960s. I remember being thrilled to see Frosty sparkle to life and then being heartbroken to see him melt away. It didn't matter that I knew he'd come back...it still hurt to see him go.

Frosty may have been just a magical story, but the idea of dying and being reborn is a difficult thing for us to understand. Frosty helped. Behind the glimmer and shimmer of Christmas is the fact that Jesus was born to die—and then to rise again. It's no magic hat that brings us back to life, though. It's a changed heart. Like snowmen, we are born dead. But like Frosty, we can dance and sing once we come to life.

We didn't have many opportunities to make snowmen down in the south. I remember being so envious of those kids up north who got to play in the snow all winter. To tell you the truth, I still am a bit miffed. Maybe I'll have the boys make me a snowman out of duck feathers this year!

1. Ephesians 2:4–5 says, "But because of his great love for us, God, who is rich in mercy, made us alive with

Christ even when we were dead in transgressions—it is by grace you have been saved." How does Christmas remind you of being reborn?

2. We could tell when Frosty came to life because his eyes changed and he began to dance and sing. What changes have you noticed in others once they have come to new life in Jesus?

3. Are there any areas of your life that feel colder than they used to? Any parts of your heart that need to come to life? Jesus is in the rebirth business all year long.

SCROOGED (1988)

STARRING: Bill Murray, Karen Allen
THEME: Transformation

For a very different take on the *Christmas Carol* story, we still like to laugh at *Scrooged*, the comedic adaptation from 1988 starring Bill Murray. As with so many '80s movies, there are a few things we would have changed if we were in charge of making the film. But this slapstick, over-the-top romp certainly taps into our collective need for personal transformation. Bill Murray makes his version of Ebenezer Scrooge despicable in very modern, relevant, and hilarious ways. We laugh, and we cringe, at the absurdity of it all. (By the way, if you watch it when it's aired on TV instead of renting a DVD, you'll enjoy it more without the ugly words, which are edited out for broadcast.)

Murray's monologue at the end is as passionate an appeal for transformation as Hollywood is able to muster. Though his Frank Cross character never specifically mentions it, we know where that miracle comes from. Yes, we need to put a little love in our hearts, but we know that we can't do that without the ultimate gift of love that first comes from God.

As Frank says, Christmas is the one time of year when people are a little nicer, a little cheerier, and a little closer to the kind, generous people that we really want to be. With Jesus in our lives, that transformation sticks around.

The light He plants in our heart just gets brighter and brighter over time.

1. Our culture is pretty comfortable talking about love, but not so comfortable talking about Jesus. In 1 John 4, though, we are told that love is from God and that everyone who loves is born of God and knows God. Have you ever taken advantage of the sentiments surrounding Christmas to talk to your neighbors, your coworkers, or maybe some lost family members about what love really is and where it comes from?

2. How has the presence of Jesus transformed you? Does your life look noticeably different from the lives of people who do not know Him?

3. If a person like Frank Cross, or Ebenezer Scrooge, was to really experience the kind of transformation depicted in this story, what would his or her life look like the day after Christmas? What "fruit" would you expect to see growing in that kind of transformed heart?

RUDOLPH THE RED-NOSED REINDEER (1964)

STARRING: Billie Mae Richards and Burl Ives
THEME: Diversity

When I was a child, I remember being completely captivated by the strangely animated annual TV special *Rudolph the Red-Nosed Reindeer.* The stop-motion animation made the whole thing look like a bunch of toys had come to life. It was a once-a-year treat that we could not wait to see.

When I watched it again after all these years, I was surprised at how oddly perfect the story actually is. Rudolph was ostracized for his glowing deformity, but as he wandered the world he found many other unique individuals. And if there has ever been a fictional land more perfect for the Robertsons than The Island of Misfit Toys, I certainly don't know what it would be.

God made each of us with special gifts. Like snowflakes, no two of us are exactly alike. The very thing you may consider a weakness or a liability may in fact be something God plans to use in a big way someday. Like the toys finding their perfect little boys and girls, or Rudolph guiding Santa's sleigh, we just have to wait for our moment to shine.

1.   Romans 8:28 promises us that God works all things for good to them that love God and are called according

to His purpose. Are there any things about your body, mind, or soul that you have felt ostracized for?

2. Describe a time when God used your uniqueness to bless someone else. How did that make them—and you—feel?

3. In 1 Corinthians 12 we are given a wonderful word picture to describe the God-designed diversity among us. Look up that passage and consider how your unique abilities, passions, and experiences can be used to bless the body of Christ.

CHRISTMAS IN CONNECTICUT (1945)
STARRING: Barbara Stanwyck, Dennis Morgan
THEME: Honesty

*C*hristmas in Connecticut is one of those romantic comedies about honesty, secrets, and consequences. You find yourself wanting to holler at the characters as they dig themselves into deeper and deeper holes. Like I told Phil, none of the drama would have happened if they would have just been honest in the first place. But I guess that's what makes a good story. As long as human beings live and move on this side of the grave, there will be dishonesty, consequences, and hilarity across the earth.

Although the story only lightly refers to Christmas, there is a subtle holiday theme that I have long suspected may have been unintentional by the writer or director. Elizabeth Lane, the focal point of the story, is a young and attractive writer whose entire career is propped up on one big lie. She has portrayed herself to be an expert cook living in the country with her husband when, in fact, she has never been married and is making up her whole persona for her readers. Of course, those plans never work out well in movies, and *Christmas in Connecticut* is no exception.

The trappings of Christmas do present us with an opportunity to reinvent ourselves a bit, don't they? I'm just glad Jesus accepts me just as I am.

1. How real are you at Christmas? Do you put forth a version of yourself that is not quite true? Why?

2. Proverbs 12:19 advises, "Truthful lips endure forever, but a lying tongue lasts only a moment." Why might we be more prone to be dishonest around the holidays? Who are we trying to impress?

3. What's the worst bit of family drama you have ever experienced around the holidays? How was it resolved, or was it?

THE GATHERING (1977)

STARRING: Edward Asner, Maureen Stapleton
THEME: Reconciliation

They sure don't make movies like *The Gathering* very often anymore. It has no special effects, crazy music, slapstick comedy—or chase scenes. It simply uses the occasion of Christmas to explore the regrets, wounds, and lingering love of one typical American family as they navigate the kind of pain that can only be inflicted by those closest to us.

Ed Asner plays Adam Thornton, a successful businessman who chooses career and autonomy over family—eventually leaving his wife Kate (Maureen Stapleton) and alienating his children. When he finds out he has terminal cancer, he decides to gather his clan for one last attempt at reconciliation. It's been years since the family has been together, and each member has his or her own reasons to fear the worst. Is it possible, though, that their love can overcome their hurt?

When I see the Thornton family, against all odds, gather together, I am reminded that the Christ Child came on a rescue mission of reconciliation. We are not meant to be alone. Nor are we meant to be separated from God. I suspect the fact that reconciliation remains such a popular theme around Christmastime is because deep down we all know how badly we need it.

1. In 2 Corinthians 5:18 we are told that Christ not only brings us reconciliation with God, but that He gives us the ministry of reconciliation to others. Is there anyone you should try to reconcile with this Christmas?

2. By all accounts Adam Thornton was a hard father to have. Why do you suppose family relationships can be so difficult to do well?

3. It took a fatal diagnosis for Adam to come to grips with the pain he had caused his wife and children. Many of us won't have advance warning when our time comes. Why do you suppose so many of us wait till the last moment to make things right? Is there anything keeping you from making those things right today?

When they saw the star,
they were overjoyed

MATTHEW 2:10

_____

8

Duck the Halls with Christmas Carols

Courtesy Russell Graves

Phil can tell you that I'm all about Christmas music. In fact, about the end of October, I get my stack of Christmas CDs out of storage and start playing them around the clock. A couple of years back, Willie and the boys thought it'd be fun to record their own album, *Duck the Halls*. Hey, even Uncle Si recorded a number. That was kind of a surreal Christmas, you know, singing along with your own Christmas CD.

Personally, I love Aaron Neville's Christmas music. I get the chills listening to his soulful voice. Willie likes to give me a hard time when I'm listening to that CD. He'll come into the kitchen and start with his lame imperson- ation of Aaron's singing—messing it up on purpose just to aggravate me. What I do to aggravate him back is the minute he walks in the door, I crank it up wide open—and play the whole CD. He'll say, "Mama, *please*." I'll not turn it off until he stops with the impersonation.

Speaking of singing, I'll never forget the year when Phil, as a leader at our church, was asked to do a little Christmas caroling with a couple of the other leaders and their spouses. Phil has never done caroling. *Never*. What happened when we got to the first house was priceless. We knocked and a lady answered, looking expectantly at this bunch of bearded carolers. Someone in the group said, "Hey, let's start with 'We Wish You a Merry Christmas.'"

Phil said, "I don't know that song."

I'm thinking, "Who doesn't know that song?"

The lady looked over at Phil. Although they'd never met, she actually said to him, "Yes, you do. You've *got* to know 'We Wish You a Merry Christmas.'"

"Nope. I don't know that song, ma'am. I don't know that song." Everybody started laughing so hard about Phil insisting he didn't know the words. Trying to defend himself, he said, "I've always *heard* it, but I've never sung that one." Phil isn't a big singer in the first place. I do love it when he sings with me, but that's about as rare as seeing an albino mallard duck. Don't get me wrong, Phil loves *hearing* Christmas music on the radio...but we were supposed to be *caroling.*

I said, "Phil, *everybody* knows that song—you just repeat the words over and over, you know?" As it turned out, Phil wouldn't sing any of the carols except for the ones that were printed on the song sheets we carried with us. Nobody bothered writing down "We Wish You a Merry Christmas" because that's such an easy one.

If you're fixin' to have a big ol' time caroling, take it from me—make the experience as painless as possible by bringing with you the lyrics to *everything* you want your group to sing. That's a surefire way to avoid the embarrassment we experienced. If caroling isn't your cup of cocoa, why not experience the joy of Christmas by singing these songs together with your family? To give you a head start, we've included the lyrics to our top ten Christmas carols.

JOY TO THE WORLD
WRITTEN BY ISAAC WATTS

Joy to the World, the Lord is come!
Let earth receive her King;
Let every heart prepare Him room,
And Heaven and nature sing,
And Heaven and nature sing,
And Heaven, and Heaven, and nature sing.

Joy to the World, the Savior reigns!
Let men their songs employ;
While fields and floods, rocks, hills, and plains
Repeat the sounding joy,
Repeat the sounding joy,
Repeat, repeat, the sounding joy.

No more let sins and sorrows grow,
Nor thorns infest the ground;
He comes to make His blessings flow
Far as the curse is found,
Far as the curse is found,
Far as, far as, the curse is found.

He rules the world with truth and grace,
And makes the nations prove
The glories of His righteousness,
And wonders of His love,
And wonders of His love,
And wonders, wonders, of His love.

JINGLE BELLS
WRITTEN BY J. PIERPONT

Dashing thro' the snow,
In a one horse open sleigh,
O'er the hills we go,
Laughing all the way;
Bells on bob tail ring,
Making spirits bright,
Oh what sport to ride and sing
A sleighing song tonight.

CHORUS:
Jingle bells, jingle bells,
Jingle all the way;
Oh! what joy it is to ride
In a one horse open sleigh.
Jingle bells, jingle bells,
Jingle all the way
Oh! what joy it is to ride
In a one horse open sleigh.

A day or two ago,
I tho't I'd take a ride;
And soon Miss Fannie Bright
Was seated by my side.
The horse was lean and lank,
Misfortune seem'd his lot:

He got into a drifted bank,
And we—we got upsot. **CHORUS**

A day or two ago,
The story I must tell;
I went out on the snow,
And on my back I fell.
A gent was riding by
In a one horse open sleigh;
He laughed as there I sprawling lie,
But quickly drove away. **CHORUS**

Now the ground is white,
Go it while you're young,
Take the girls tonight
And sing this sleighing song;
Just get a bob tailed bay,
Two forty as his speed;
Hitch him to an open sleigh,
And crack, you'll take the lead. **CHORUS**

SILENT NIGHT
WRITTEN BY JOSEPH MOHR AND JOHN YOUNG

Silent night, holy night!
All is calm, all is bright.
Round yon virgin, mother and child.
Holy infant, tender and mild,
Sleep in heavenly peace,
Sleep in heavenly peace.

Silent night, holy night!
Shepherds quake, at the sight.
Glories stream from heaven above,
Heavenly hosts sing, "Alleluia!
Christ the Savior is born,
Christ the Savior is born."

Silent night, holy night!
Son of God, love's pure light.
Radiant beams from Thy holy face,
With the dawn of redeeming grace,
Jesus, Lord at Thy birth,
Jesus, Lord at Thy birth.

THE TWELVE DAYS OF CHRISTMAS

AUTHOR UNKNOWN

On the first day of Christmas
my true love sent to me:
A Partridge in a Pear Tree.

On the second day of Christmas
my true love sent to me:
Two Turtle Doves,
and a Partridge in a Pear Tree.

On the third day of Christmas
my true love sent to me:
Three French Hens,
Two Turtle Doves,
and a Partridge in a Pear Tree.

On the fourth day of Christmas
my true love sent to me:
Four Calling Birds,
Three French Hens,
Two Turtle Doves,
and a Partridge in a Pear Tree.

On the fifth day of Christmas
my true love sent to me:
Five Golden Rings,
Four Calling Birds,

Three French Hens,
Two Turtle Doves,
and a Partridge in a Pear Tree.

On the sixth day of Christmas
my true love sent to me:
Six Geese a Laying,
Five Golden Rings,
Four Calling Birds,
Three French Hens,
Two Turtle Doves,
and a Partridge in a Pear Tree.

On the seventh day of Christmas
my true love sent to me:
Seven Swans a Swimming,
Six Geese a Laying,
Five Golden Rings,
Four Calling Birds,
Three French Hens,
Two Turtle Doves,
and a Partridge in a Pear Tree.

On the eighth day of Christmas
my true love sent to me:
Eight Maids a Milking,
Seven Swans a Swimming,
Six Geese a Laying,
Five Golden Rings,

Four Calling Birds,
Three French Hens,
Two Turtle Doves,
and a Partridge in a Pear Tree.

On the ninth day of Christmas
my true love sent to me:
Nine Ladies Dancing,
Eight Maids a Milking,
Seven Swans a Swimming,
Six Geese a Laying,
Five Golden Rings,
Four Calling Birds,
Three French Hens,
Two Turtle Doves,
and a Partridge in a Pear Tree.

On the tenth day of Christmas
my true love sent to me:
Ten Lords a Leaping,
Nine Ladies Dancing,
Eight Maids a Milking,
Seven Swans a Swimming,
Six Geese a Laying,
Five Golden Rings,
Four Calling Birds,
Three French Hens,
Two Turtle Doves,
and a Partridge in a Pear Tree.

On the eleventh day of Christmas
my true love sent to me:
Eleven Pipers Piping,
Ten Lords a Leaping,
Nine Ladies Dancing,
Eight Maids a Milking,
Seven Swans a Swimming,
Six Geese a Laying,
Five Golden Rings,
Four Calling Birds,
Three French Hens,
Two Turtle Doves,
and a Partridge in a Pear Tree.

On the twelfth day of Christmas
my true love sent to me:
Twelve Drummers Drumming,
Eleven Pipers Piping,
Ten Lords a Leaping,
Nine Ladies Dancing,
Eight Maids a Milking,
Seven Swans a Swimming,
Six Geese a Laying,
Five Golden Rings,
Four Calling Birds,
Three French Hens,
Two Turtle Doves,
and a Partridge in a Pear Tree.

HARK! THE HERALD ANGELS SING
WRITTEN BY CHARLES WESLEY, GEORGE WHITEFIELD, AND MARTIN MADAN

Hark! The herald angels sing,
"Glory to the newborn King;
Peace on earth and mercy mild;
God and sinners reconciled."
Joyful all ye nations rise,
Join the triumph of the skies;
With th'angelic host proclaim,
"Christ is born in Bethlehem!"

CHORUS:
Hark! The herald angels sing,
"Glory to the newborn King!"

Christ by highest heaven adored;
Christ, the everlasting Lord;
Late in time behold He'll come,
Offspring of a Virgin's womb.
Veiled in flesh the Godhead see;
Hail the incarnate deity,
Pleased as man with man to dwell,
Jesus, our Emmanuel. CHORUS

Hail, the heaven born Prince of Peace!
Hail, the Son of Righteousness!
Light and life to all He brings,

Risen with healing in His wings.
Mild He lays His glory by,
Born that man no more may die;
Born to raise the sons of earth,
Born to give them second birth. CHORUS

O COME, ALL YE FAITHFUL
WRITTEN BY JOHN FRANCIS WADE AND FREDERICK OAKELEY

O come, all ye faithful, joyful and triumphant!
Oh come ye, O come ye, to Bethlehem!
Come and behold Him, born the King of angels;

CHORUS:
O come, let us adore Him,
O come, let us adore Him,
O come, let us adore Him,
Christ the Lord.

God of God, light of light
Lo He not the virgin's womb;
Very God begotten not created. CHORUS

Sing, choirs of angels, sing in exultation,
Sing, all ye citizens of heaven above;
Glory to God in the highest. CHORUS

See how the shepherds summoned to His cradle,
leaving their flocks, draw nigh with lowly fear
we too will thither hend our joyful footsteps. CHORUS

Yea, Lord, we greet thee, born this happy morning;
Jesus, to thee be glory given;
Word of the Father, now in flesh appearing. CHORUS

DECK THE HALLS
WRITTEN BY THOMAS OLIPHANT

Deck the halls with boughs of holly,
Fa la la la la, la la la la.
'Tis the season to be jolly,
Fa la la la la, la la la la.

Don we now our gay apparel,
Fa la la, la la la, la la la.
Troll the ancient Yule tide carol,
Fa la la la la, la la la la.

See the blazing Yule before us,
Fa la la la la, la la la la.
Strike the harp and join the chorus.
Fa la la la la, la la la la.

Follow me in merry measure,
Fa la la la la, la la la la.
While I tell of Yule tide treasure,
Fa la la la la, la la la la.

Fast away the old year passes,
Fa la la la la, la la la la.
Hail the new, ye lads and lasses,
Fa la la la la, la la la la.
Sing we joyous, all together,
Fa la la la la, la la la la.

Heedless of the wind and weather,
Fa la la la la, la la la la.

AWAY IN A MANGER
AUTHOR UNKNOWN

Away in a manger,
No crib for a bed,
The little Lord Jesus
Laid down His sweet head.
The stars in the sky
Looked down where He lay,
The little Lord Jesus
Asleep on the hay.

The cattle are lowing,
The Baby awakes.
The little Lord Jesus,
No crying He makes.
I love Thee, Lord Jesus,
Look down from the sky,
And stay by my cradle
till morning is nigh.

Be near me, Lord Jesus,
I ask Thee to stay
Close by me forever,
And love me I pray.
Bless all the dear children
In Thy tender care,
And take us for heaven
To live with Thee there.

THE FIRST NOEL
AUTHOR UNKNOWN

The First Noel, the Angels did say,
Was to certain poor shepherds in fields as they lay;
In fields where they lay keeping their sheep,
On a cold winter's night that was so deep.

CHORUS:
Noel, Noel, Noel, Noel
Born is the King of Israel!

They looked up and saw a star
Shining in the East beyond them far;
And to the earth it gave great light,
And so it continued both day and night. CHORUS

And by the light of that same star,
Three Wise men came from country far
To seek for a King was their intent,
And to follow the star wherever it went. CHORUS

This star drew nigh to the northwest,
O'er Bethlehem it took its rest;
And there it did both stop and stay;
Right o'er the place where Jesus lay. CHORUS

Then entered in those Wise men three,
Full reverently upon their knee,

And offered there in His presence,
Their gold and myrrh and frankincense. CHORUS

Then let us all with one accord
Sing praises to our heavenly Lord
That hath made Heaven and earth of nought,
And with His blood mankind has bought. CHORUS

HALLELUJAH CHORUS
WRITTEN BY GEORGE FRIEDRICH HANDEL

Hallelujah! Hallelujah! Hallelujah! Halleluja!
Hallelujah!
Hallelujah! Hallelujah! Hallelujah! Halleluja!
Hallelujah!

For the Lord God omnipotent reigneth.
Hallelujah! Hallelujah! Hallelujah! Halleluja!
For the Lord God omnipotent reigneth.
Hallelujah! Hallelujah! Hallelujah! Halleluja!
For the Lord God omnipotent reigneth.
Hallelujah! Hallelujah! Hallelujah! Halleluja!

Hallelujah! Hallelujah! Hallelujah! Halleluja!
Hallelujah! Hallelujah! Hallelujah! Halleluja!
(For the Lord God omnipotent reigneth.)
Hallelujah! Hallelujah! Hallelujah! Halleluja!

For the Lord God omnipotent reigneth.
(Hallelujah! Hallelujah! Hallelujah! Halleluja!)
Hallelujah!

The kingdom of this world;
is become
the kingdom of our Lord,
and of His Christ,

and of His Christ,
And He shall reign forever and ever,
And He shall reign forever and ever,
And He shall reign forever and ever,
And He shall reign forever and ever.

King of kings forever and ever. Hallelujah! Hallelujah!
And lord of lords forever and ever. Hallelujah!
Hallelujah!
King of kings forever and ever. Hallelujah! Hallelujah!
And lord of lords forever and ever. Hallelujah!
Hallelujah!
King of kings forever and ever. Hallelujah! Hallelujah!
And lord of lords.
King of kings and lord of lords.

And He shall reign,
And He shall reign,
And He shall reign,
He shall reign,
And He shall reign forever and ever.

King of kings forever and ever,
and lord of lords. Hallelujah! Hallelujah!
And He shall reign forever and ever.

King of kings and lord of lords.
King of kings and lord of lords.

And He shall reign forever and ever.

Forever and ever and ever and ever.
(King of kings and lord of lords.)
Hallelujah! Hallelujah! Hallelujah! Hallelujah!
Hallelujah!

*Therefore the Lord himself
will give you a sign: The virgin
will conceive and give birth
to a son, and will call him
Immanuel.*

ISAIAH 7:14

9

Have Yourself a Merry Cajun Christmas

On Christmas Day, most folks in Yuppieville have a turkey, a ham, a roast, or whatnot ready to go from the supermarket. Not me. I'm in the duck blind first thing Christmas morning. Although I've got standby ducks ready in case I come up empty handed, I prefer to harvest the ducks for our main meal on Christmas, which is around two o'clock. I like to get a big roaster pan to make a huge dish of preferably green-winged teal or wood ducks. I'll bring them in, clean them, and boil them. You don't want to boil them until they fall to pieces. Boil them to where they're real tender—until the leg will pull off. You don't want them falling apart.

Miss Kay likes it when I save the broth for the dressing. She makes the cornbread and I make a cornbread dressing from it. I'll strategically arrange the ducks in a big round circle with a couple, maybe three, woodies placed in the middle. I'll nestle the ducks I shot in about an inch or so of dressing. It is one of the finest meals you'll ever eat. We'll serve them with a side of cranberry sauce. But that's just a part of our Cajun Christmas meal.

For an appetizer, Miss Kay used to make a beer batter–dipped shrimp—the key phrase here is "*used to* make." One Christmas she and a couple of the women were frying up the battered shrimp in the kitchen. When I got back from the duck blind, I walked in there to sample some of the fruit of their labors. I mean to tell you, the batter was so thick—and there was so much of it—I couldn't even find the shrimp up under all of that batter. It was just coming out of the frying pan in big blobs of dough.

I was trying to eat them but ended up with a mouthful of fried batter.

I walked over to the stove and said, "I have an announcement to make." Miss Kay and the women gave me a look. I said, "From now on, *I* will fry all the shrimp. You are relieved of your command. You are removed from your duties of having to cook shrimp at Christmas." With a wink, Miss Kay said, "Well, thank you, Phil. Let's see if you can do better."

I said, "Look, I don't know what mad scientist dreamed up that recipe, but beer-battered shrimp ain't the way to go. Trust me, I can beat this." That's when I started frying them. And now everybody is happy, happy, happy. If you're going to feed twelve or fifteen people, take about 5 pounds of fresh shrimp, those medium-sized ones. You peel them, de-head them, and split them down the middle. You've got to devein them—you know, take that vein out of them, or buy them that way. Put a little salt—I'm talking a very little salt—some garlic powder, and black pepper, and then roll them around. Take a whisk and whisk about 6 to 8 eggs. Whisk them real good. Get them all beat up and then pour the eggs over the shrimp. Roll them around in that egg wash.

Then, start getting your grease good and hot. Meanwhile, take about 3 sifters full of flour. You roll them shrimp up in that flour until they separate from each other. You don't want them gloppy. If they're sticking together, put in more flour until they separate. Then drop them into hot peanut or canola oil and take them out after 1 minute—but no more. Trust me, they're ready to go in less than a minute, even medium-sized shrimp. Once you take them out of there, put the shrimp on the platter and sprinkle with whatever essence you want—be it Cajun spice or whatever.

That's the way you fry shrimp, Jack. They'll turn out perfect every time. Stay off the beer batter, see what I'm saying? I had to move in on Miss Kay's turf twenty years ago, and I've been frying them since then. Now everyone says they're the best thing they've ever put in their mouth. Don't you know ever since I brought up that story I'm hungry for them! While you try your hand at that dish, here are a couple of other Christmas menu items from the Robertson household.

PHIL'S FAMOUS HOT COCOA
MAKES 4 SERVINGS

Medium saucepan
1 cup unsweetened cocoa powder
½ cup sugar
Pinch of salt
1 cup hot water
1 quart milk
¾ teaspoon vanilla extract

1. In a medium saucepan, stir together the cocoa powder, sugar, and salt. Add the water, stirring to moisten the cocoa. Bring to a boil over medium heat. Boil, stirring constantly, for 2 minutes.

2. Add the milk, stir, and heat until just steaming (do not boil after adding the milk). Stir in the vanilla and serve.

CRESCENT ROLL WREATH APPETIZER
MAKES 8 TO 12 SERVINGS

12- to 14-inch pizza pan
Cooking spray
8 ounces chive and onion cream cheese, at room
   temperature
1 cup finely chopped fresh or thawed frozen broccoli
   florets
½ cup finely chopped red bell pepper
¼ cup finely chopped water chestnuts
2 tablespoons finely chopped green onions (scallions)
¼ cup finely chopped baked ham or crisp-cooked
   bacon (optional)
Salt and black pepper
2 cans (8 ounces each) refrigerated crescent roll dough
1 large egg
1 tablespoon cold water
2 teaspoons sesame seeds

1. Preheat the oven to 375°F. Mist a 12- to 14-inch pizza
pan with cooking spray.

2. In a medium bowl, stir together the cream cheese,
broccoli, bell pepper, water chestnuts, green onions, and
ham or bacon (if using). Season with salt and pepper to
taste.

3. Unwrap the crescent roll dough and separate along the perforations into 16 triangles. Arrange the triangles in a circle with the wide sides toward the center and the long, tapered points facing out over the edge of the pan; leave a 5-inch-wide open space in the center. Let the edges of the wide sides overlap slightly and gently press them together.

4. Spoon the cream cheese mixture onto the widest part of the circle of dough. Pull the long points of dough over the filling and tuck under the ends to form a ring. Some of the filling will remain visible between the strips of dough. The finished round should resemble a wreath.

5. Whisk together the egg and water. Brush the dough with the egg mixture and sprinkle with the sesame seeds. Bake until the dough is deep golden brown, 20 to 25 minutes. Cool on the pan for 5 minutes. Run a metal spatula under the wreath and then slide it onto a serving platter. Slice and serve warm or at room temperature.

FESTIVE HOLIDAY CHEESE BALL
MAKES 12 SERVINGS

2 packages (8 ounces each) cream cheese, at room
    temperature
2 teaspoons Worcestershire sauce
1 teaspoon garlic powder
1 teaspoon hot sauce, or to taste
1 teaspoon lemon juice
8 ounces extra-sharp cheddar cheese, grated (about 2
    cups)
2 tablespoons finely chopped green onions (scallions)
2 tablespoons finely chopped red bell pepper
2 cups salted or smoked whole almonds
1 or 2 short, full sprigs fresh rosemary, for garnish
Good crackers, for serving

1. In a large bowl, stir together the cream cheese, Worcestershire sauce, garlic powder, hot sauce, and lemon juice
until smooth. Stir in the cheese, green onions, and bell
pepper.

2. Scrape the mixture onto a large sheet of plastic wrap.
Form into a tapered triangle with rounded corners to
resemble a pinecone. Starting at the tapered end, arrange the
almonds in parallel rows over the top and side of the cheese

mixture, slightly overlapping the points and positioning them to look like the scales of a pinecone. Wrap in the plastic wrap and refrigerate until firm.

3. Let sit at room temperature for 20 minutes before serving. Just before serving, insert the rosemary in the top to look like greenery. Serve with crackers.

Courtesy Russell Graves

CRAB SPREAD
MAKES 12 TO 16 SERVINGS

Large saucepan
2 tablespoons butter
2 green onions (scallions), finely chopped (about 2
    tablespoons)
¼ cup finely chopped red bell pepper
8 ounces cream cheese
1 tablespoon mayonnaise
1 tablespoon Dijon mustard
1 teaspoon Worcestershire sauce
½ teaspoon salt, or to taste
¼ teaspoon black pepper, or to taste
1 teaspoon hot sauce, or to taste
2 teaspoons Old Bay seasoning, plus more for
    sprinkling
2 tablespoons finely chopped flat-leaf parsley
12 ounces lump crabmeat, picked through for bits of
    shell
1 to 4 tablespoons heavy cream, as needed
Toasted baguette slices or good crackers, for serving

1. In a large saucepan, melt the butter over medium-high
heat. Add the green onions and bell pepper and cook, stirring often, until tender, about 5 minutes.

2. Add the cream cheese, mayonnaise, mustard, Worcestershire sauce, salt, pepper, hot sauce, Old Bay, and parsley and mix well. Cook over medium-low heat until heated through.

3. Fold in the crabmeat. If the mixture is too thick, stir in heavy cream as needed. Season with more salt and pepper to taste.

4. Sprinkle with Old Bay and serve warm with baguette slices or crackers.

Courtesy Russell Graves

CRAWFISH PIE
MAKES 1 (9-INCH) PIE

Large skillet
9-inch pie pan
1 stick (¼ pound) butter
1 small onion, finely chopped
1 bell pepper, finely chopped
1 celery stalk, finely chopped
2 tablespoons all-purpose flour
1 can (10.75 ounces) cream of mushroom soup
Pinch each of salt and black pepper
Duck Commander Cajun Seasoning (mild or zesty)
1 pound crawfish tail meat, fresh or thawed frozen
2 (9-inch) piecrusts, homemade or store-bought,
    unbaked

1. Preheat the oven to 350°F.

2. In the skillet, melt the butter over medium heat. Add the onion, bell pepper, and celery and cook, stirring occasionally, until very soft, 15 to 20 minutes.

3. Add the flour and stir until the vegetables are coated well. Stir in the soup, salt, pepper, Cajun seasoning, and crawfish tails.

4. Fit one piece of dough into the pie pan, pressing it into the sides to prevent it from slipping down. Bake for 5 minutes, then remove it from the oven.

5. Spoon the crawfish filling into the crust and top with the remaining dough. Pinch the edges together. With a knife, make several slashes in the top for steam vents.

6. Bake until the crust is golden brown and the filling is bubbling, about 30 minutes.

~~~~~~

Miss Kay says . . .

I've been blessed with a husband and four sons who love to hunt and fish. Maybe you have outdoorsmen in your family, too. If not, no problem. You can still treat your family to this unique Christmas dish using frozen crawfish. Trust me, they'll work just fine.

PHIL'S DUCK GUMBO
MAKES 10 TO 15 SERVINGS

Large (10- to 14-quart) soup pot with a lid

Large (7- to 8-quart) cooking pot

4 wood ducks or 6 teal or 3 mallards; plucked, eviscerated, and cleaned; heads and feet removed

Salt and black pepper

3 bay leaves

2 cups peanut oil

2 cups all-purpose flour

3 white onions, chopped

3 green onions (scallions), chopped

3 celery stalks, chopped

6 garlic cloves, chopped

A handful of fresh parsley, chopped

Duck Commander Cajun Seasoning (mild or zesty) or other Cajun seasoning

1 package (24 ounces) hot pork sausage, diced nickel-size (we use Savoie's)

1 package (24 ounces) Andouille sausage, diced nickel-size

1 package (28 ounces) frozen whole okra

1. Place the ducks in the soup pot filled with water. Add the salt and pepper to taste, and the bay leaves. Bring to a boil, lower to a simmer, and cook until the ducks are tender but not falling apart, about two hours.

2. Remove the ducks from the broth and set aside. Reserve the broth (discard the bay leaves). When the ducks are cool enough to handle, skin them and remove the meat from the bones; discard the skin and bones.

3. While your ducks are cooking, in the large cooking pot, heat the oil over medium-low heat. Add the flour and cook, stirring frequently, until the roux is a dark chocolate color, 35 to 40 minutes.

4. Add the white and green onions, celery, garlic, and parsley to the roux. Add enough of the reserved broth to fill it just over half-full, and bring it to a boil. Skim off any oil that rises to the surface.

5. Add the Cajun seasoning along with the hot pork sausage, Andouille, and duck meat. Simmer two hours, then add the okra and simmer 1 hour longer, or until all the meat is tender and the gumbo has thickened.

BROCCOLI AND RICE CASSEROLE
MAKES 12 SERVINGS

9x13-inch baking dish
Cooking spray
2 tablespoons butter
1 cup finely chopped celery
1 cup finely chopped onion
1 can (10.75 ounces) condensed cream of mushroom
  soup
1 can (10.75 ounces) condensed cream of celery soup
1 can (12 ounces) evaporated milk
1 loaf (16 ounces) Velveeta, cut into 1-inch cubes
1 teaspoon salt
½ teaspoon black pepper
4 cups cooked and cooled chopped broccoli
3 cups cooked and cooled long-grain white rice

1. Preheat the oven to 350°F. Mist a 9x13-inch baking dish
with cooking spray.

2. In a large saucepan, melt the butter over medium-
high heat. Add the celery and onion and cook, stirring
occasionally, until tender, about 5 minutes.

3. Stir in the cream of mushroom soup, cream of celery
soup, and evaporated milk, and stir until well mixed. Bring

to a simmer, add the Velveeta, and cook, stirring constantly, until melted and smooth. Stir in the salt, pepper, broccoli, and rice.

4. Pour into the baking dish and bake until golden brown and bubbling, about 45 minutes. Let stand 10 minutes before serving warm.

Courtesy Russell Graves

BLACKBERRY JAM CAKE
MAKES 1 (9X13-INCH) CAKE

9x13-inch cake pan
Electric mixer
Medium saucepan
Nonstick cooking spray and flour, for the pan
Cake
2 cups sugar
2 sticks (½ pound) butter, softened (do not use
    margarine)
4 large eggs, separated
1 teaspoon vanilla extract
3 cups all-purpose flour
1 teaspoon baking soda
2 teaspoons ground cinnamon
1 teaspoon grated nutmeg
1 teaspoon ground cloves
1 teaspoon ground allspice
1 cup buttermilk
1 cup blackberry jam
Caramel Frosting
1 cup whole milk
1 cup evaporated milk (I use Pet)
2 cups sugar
2 tablespoons butter
1 teaspoon vanilla extract
1 cup candied cherries
1 cup coarsely chopped nuts (we like pecans or walnuts)

1. Preheat the oven to 425°F. Grease and flour the cake pan.

2. Make the cake: In a large bowl, with the electric mixer, beat the sugar and butter until creamy.

3. Add egg yolks and vanilla and beat until blended.

4. Sift together the flour, baking soda, cinnamon, nutmeg, cloves, and allspice. Add the flour mixture and buttermilk alternately to the creamed butter, beginning and ending with the flour.

5. Add the blackberry jam and mix well.

6. In a separate bowl, beat the egg whites to stiff peaks with the mixer. (The peaks will stay standing when you remove the beaters.) Gently fold into the batter.

7. Pour the batter into the pan. Bake until the cake starts to pull away at the sides and a toothpick inserted in the center comes out clean, about 40 minutes.

8. Let the cake cool in the pan for a few minutes, then run a spatula around the sides and invert onto a wire rack to cool completely.

9. Make the frosting: Cook the whole and evaporated milks, sugar, and butter in the saucepan over medium heat, stirring constantly, until a soft ball forms. Stir in the vanilla, cherries, and nuts. Frost the cake immediately, before the caramel hardens.

Courtesy Russell Graves

GRANDMA'S FRUIT CAKE

MAKES 1 CAKE

10-inch stem cake pan
Electric mixer
3 large bowls
Nonstick cooking spray and flour, for the pan
Dry Ingredients
1 pound sweet cream butter
1 pound brown sugar
7 eggs
5 cups all-purpose flour
1 teaspoon baking soda
1 teaspoon nutmeg
1 tablespoon mace
1 tablespoon cinnamon
Fruit and Nut Ingredients
1 pound raisins
1 pound currants (optional)
2 pounds candied cherries
2 pounds candied pineapple
1 pound citrus
1 pound dates
1 pound mixed candied fruit
3 or 4 pounds nuts mixed (whole)

1. Preheat the oven to 300°F. Grease and lightly flour the stem cake pan.

2. In a large bowl, cream butter until soft and smooth. Gradually stir in brown sugar.

3. Add the 7 eggs, one at a time, beating well after each egg is added.

4. In a separate bowl, sift together flour, baking soda, nutmeg, mace, and cinnamon.

5. Add half of the flour mixture to the butter and sugar mixture.

6. In a third bowl, take raisins, currants, cherries, pineapple, citrus, dates, candied fruit, and nuts and blend well with the remaining half of the flour mixture.

7. Combine with the butter and sugar mixture, then pour dough into the greased and floured stem pan.

8. Bake 3 to 4 hours at 300°F, or until cake leaves sides of pan; cool overnight before removing from pan.

For God so loved the world that he gave his one and only Son, that whoever believes in him shall not perish but have eternal life.

JOHN 3:16

10

The Phil of Christmas Past, Present, and Future

Way back in the early 1800s, there lived a twelve-year-old boy whose daddy was thrown into the debtors' prison due to amassing a pile of unpaid bills. His momma got the notion to move his family into the prison, too. She reckoned that way they could still be together as a family with their father. Hey, I guess in those days that was a viable option. She also made plans to farm out her son to work in a dingy warehouse pasting labels on glass bottles and whatnot.

You've got to remember this was long before child labor laws existed. Separated from his family, the boy slaved away in ungodly conditions alongside other youngsters. This traumatic arrangement lasted for something like three months, after which time his father was released. Reunited with his family, the boy returned to school—but the emotional impact of that experience was seared into his memory.

He went on to become a law clerk, a court reporter, and ultimately a world-renowned English novelist who penned one of the most moving Christmas stories ever. I think it was highly unlikely that old Charles Dickens had any earthly idea how his little novella *A Christmas Carol* would impact the world. I mean, Dickens gave us the miserly Ebenezer Scrooge with his "Bah! Humbug!"; the faithful yet poor-as-dirt Bob Cratchit; his crippled son, Tiny Tim; and the unforgettable three visiting spirits of Christmas past, present, and future. That story got me to thinking about my Christmases past, present, and future—no doubt that sort of soul searching was what Dickens had intended his novel to do.

Let me take you back to the "Phil of Christmas Past."

When I was a child, things were pretty rustic growing up in the old Robertson household. It might have been the 1950s, but we lived in a three-room log cabin as if the clock had been turned back a hundred years. Things got worse when my daddy fell off of an oil derrick. He broke his back and was out of commission for close to three years. That meant that every time Christmas rolled around, we had nothing. Hey, financially speaking we were doing so badly we couldn't afford one of those Charlie Brown–sized Christmas trees, see what I'm saying?

And yet, even though I was just a boy, something registered inside of me that Christmas was a big deal and worthy of celebration. So when I was hunting squirrels during the fall, I'd mark the trees that I thought might make a good Christmas tree. Later I'd go back and chop one down and drag it home. As Christmas approached, I hunted ducks and geese, which were the food we ate on Christmas Day.

As I grew older, my poverty wasn't just in the area of finances. I was spiritually poor. We celebrated Christmas with what we had, but the birth of Jesus didn't impact my heart. In junior high, eighth grade probably, one of my buddies must of noticed because he said, "Phil, let's go to church and get baptized." Trust me when I tell you I had no idea why—I just went out and did it. I was too young to understand the implications of all of that. I had no idea what I was doing. I just went into that old church and I got wet when they dunked me in that baptismal font.

From about age fifteen to age twenty-eight, having fallen victim to the current culture, which, at that time, was characterized by sex, drugs, and rock and roll, I went on a substantial terror. You see what I'm saying? Sure, I went to college on a football scholarship, but that's where the old Phil really started sinning in earnest—getting drunk, smoking dope, fighting, and carrying on all that stuff. I didn't know it at the time, but during my romping and stomping days, I was living in line with what the Apostle Paul described as the "acts of the flesh" in Galatians 5:19–21:

> The acts of the flesh are obvious: sexual immorality, impurity and debauchery; idolatry and witchcraft; hatred, discord, jealousy, fits of rage, selfish ambition, dissensions, factions and envy; drunkenness, orgies, and the like. I warn you, as I did before, that those who live like this will not inherit the kingdom of God.

This list is an exact explanation of who I was back then. Mind you, I wasn't guilty of all of them, but during this period in my life I wasn't on board with Jesus. As they say, "The proof is in the pudding," and all I had to do was to look at my behavior to see I was in a serious dither. In light of the list Paul put together, this was my identity at the time:

"Sexual immorality"—guilty as charged.

"Impurity"—guilty as charged.

"Debauchery"—yup, in spades.

"Idolatry"—guilty.

"Witchcraft"—I was not into witchcraft.

"Hatred"—yes, sir.

"Discord"—yup.

"Jealousy"—big time.

"Fits of rage"—all of the time.

"Selfish ambition"—I'm not sure about that one.

"Dissentions"—oh, yeah.

"Factions and envy"—not so much.

"Drunkenness"—oh, right at the top of the list.

"Orgies"—yup.

The Apostle Paul went on to say, "I warn you, as I did before, that those who live like this will not inherit the kingdom." I mean to tell you, although I made a point to celebrate Christmas, I had no part of the inheritance of the kingdom of God. None. I didn't know that I was in such a bind. I didn't know I was blind. I didn't know I was a child of the devil until later, when I looked back at the way I was living. I was under the control of the devil until I was twenty-eight years old. I was producing the fruit of the devil. He was working in me. I was his prisoner. Paul writes, "The god of this age has blinded the minds of unbelievers, so that they cannot see the light of the gospel that displays the glory of Christ, who is the image of God" (2 Corinthians 4:4).

That was me.

I had been taken captive. I was living in darkness.

Which is why the "Phil of Christmas Past" produced the worst Christmas in memory for Miss Kay and the boys. This would have been 1974. In addition to my personal evil ways, I was in trouble with the law and lived in the woods for several months trying to evade the police. I ended up working in the oil fields offshore down on the Gulf of Mexico. Meanwhile, Miss Kay moved to Farmerville, Louisiana, to get away from all of those troubles and the rednecks I had been partying with.

That year was such a sad Christmas for my family.

You might say it was our worst Christmas ever.

Complicating matters, we were dirt poor. Although we were apart, Miss Kay tried to make the best of Christmas by buying little cheap gadgets and widgets and plastic trinkets from the grocery store so the boys would have something to open for Christmas morning. That's all she could afford. Unbeknown to me, the greatest gift she had been working on was the way she was fighting to save our marriage. She told the boys, "That's not your daddy. That's the devil in your daddy."

You see, during those dark days when we all hit rock bottom, Miss Kay saw a preacher, William "Bill" Smith, pastor of White's Ferry Road Church, on the television.

He was talking about how to get true peace and hope and joy. She called and made an appointment to see him. After sharing the good news that she could have Jesus Christ living inside of her heart, she confessed her need for a Savior, repented of her sin, and was baptized. She left his office a new person.

That wasn't good news as far as I was concerned.

I had no use for her Jesus. None.

I called her a "holy roller" and a "Bible thumper." Hey, I was such a mess that, after accusing her of all manner of things—including having an affair on me—none of which was true, I ran Miss Kay and the boys out of the house. She ended up in a little bitty low-rent apartment partially subsidized by the church—but she never gave up on me. Now, fast-forward three months. When I finally came to the end of my rope, I pulled my pickup truck into the parking lot where Miss Kay was working and just wept. I was done with the old Phil. One problem.

I didn't know what to do about it.

Miss Kay took me to meet with Pastor Bill. I confess I didn't trust that dude as far as I could throw him. But I did trust whatever was written in the Bible. So Bill and I studied that thing for several hours. When we were finished, I said, "This just seems too good to be true. You mean to tell me that Jesus was born on Christmas, He grew up and lived perfectly—zero mistakes—and then He died for a wayward rascal like me so I can live eternally with Him? Good grief!"

Bill assured me it was all true. I said, "Look, preacher, I don't want to hurt your feelings but I'll have to double-check stuff. I'm sitting on a Master's degree so I've gotta check this out to make sure what you have said is accurate." I mean, to be pulled out of Satan's clutches...to be free from living under Satan's control...to have all of my sins washed away—gone for good...to be free from my guilt and shame...and to have a way out of the grave into heaven, man, that was too good to be true.

How I missed that amazing news all of those years I'll never know.

I might have celebrated Christmas, but I was just a dead man walking. Once I put it all together and researched every word to make sure it was correct, I called that preacher back and told him I was done rejecting God's gift and His purpose for my life. Just like Miss Kay, I repented, I confessed my sins, I was baptized, and I was raised up in new life in Jesus. No question, a genuine transformation took place in my heart.

Which brings me to the "Phil of Christmas Present."

At age twenty-eight, I was born again, not of my mother, like the first birth. This time I was born of water and the Spirit of God. Look, the first me was filled with sexual immorality, impurity, debauchery, idolatry, hatred, discord, jealously, and fits of rage. The second me is filled with love, joy, peace, patience, kindness, goodness, faithfulness, gentleness, and self-control. Which is why if you were to ask Miss Kay what was her best Christmas ever, she'd tell you it was the year I gave my heart to Jesus. We may have been living in that tiny apartment with a handful of presents and a few dollars to our name, but it was the first year I allowed the power of the Christ Child to transform my heart. We were rich beyond any material possession.

So while folks scurry about shopping, decorating, eating, and whatnot at Christmas, I'm reminded of how desperately I needed Jesus, and how different I am today than I was with my old heathen identity. Just as Scrooge changed his life after being visited by the spirits in *A Christmas Carol*, I changed my ways after the Holy Spirit got ahold of me. Maybe old Dickens was preaching the gospel in his own way, right? Which leads me to the best part of all. You say, "What could be better than being forgiven and transformed into a new person free of the bondage of sin?" I'll tell you.

A day is coming when I, and all of those who place their faith in Jesus, will be celebrating Christmas with Jesus, the Prince of Peace Himself. It's an undeniable fact that the "Phil of Christmas Future" will be eternally happy, happy, happy because of His incredible promise: "No longer will there be any curse. The throne of God and of the Lamb will be in the city, and his servants will serve him. They will see his face, and his name will be on their foreheads. There will be no more night. They will not need the light of a lamp or the light of the sun, for the Lord God will give them light. And they will reign for ever and ever" (Revelation 22:3–5).

Reigning *with* Jesus? No gift can compare with that. Think about it. Without Jesus there is no Christmas. Without Christmas there is no Easter. Without Easter there is no resurrection from the dead and no removal of our guilt and sin. And without a resurrection, there's no life eternal in heaven, see what I'm saying? Given what's at stake, for the life of me I can't figure out why everybody doesn't follow Jesus.

You've just heard the greatest news ever.

Why not move on it like we did?

ALSO BY Miss Kay

Available wherever books are sold
or at SimonandSchuster.com